Become a Podmaster

Become a Podmaster

Everything You Need to Know to Master
the Art of Podcasting

Hendrik Baird

Baird Media Publishing

BAIRD MEDIA PUBLISHING

Published by Baird Media (Pty) Ltd.

1090 Cura Avenue, Equestria, Pretoria, Gauteng, 0184, Republic of South Africa.

https://baird.media

First published by Baird Media (Pty) Ltd (Publishing) 2023.

ISBN: 978-0-6397-6788-8 (print)

          978-0-6397-6789-5 (e-book)

What People Say About This Book

"Hendrik Baird is a meticulous writer and a valued insightful contributor to the broadcasting landscape.

"I've been podcasting for just over a decade and train broadcasters. I learnt so many integral and stand-out insights to the podcasting medium reading this.

"Podcasting is a growing and volatile space, and this guide is exactly what everyone needs when deciding to tell their own story within the podcasting realm."

Chris Jordan

https://chrisjordanmedia.net/

"This book is an outstanding resource. It is a comprehensive look at podcasting, which is not only helpful for the beginner, but also for the person who has been podcasting but wants to take it to the next level.

"Thank you so much for sharing this with me. I will be using it as we look to re-establish our podcast and create new ones."

Oliver Marcelle

https://www.denoli.org/

"I love the format of the book and that you give Action Steps. You also give some ideas for platforms and why you think they're the best! Great job!"

Sondra Ray

https://ray-va.com/

"Hendrik says this is not a step-by-step guide to podcasting, but I would perhaps challenge that as this book provides everything you need to know on this popular topic.

"It is a comprehensive guide that takes you through all the important decisions you will need to make to create a successful podcast, from a deep dive into your ideal listener to how to find these listeners when you have your finished podcast ready to launch.

"This book will definitely help you kickstart your podcasting career."

Rhona McCormick

https://www.linkedin.com/in/rhona-maccormick-transform-content-marketing/

"Hendrik is a masterful storyteller and clearly also knowledgeable about the world of podcasting. I learnt so much I never even knew I needed to learn to be a podmaster! I am so thankful that he took the time to write this pocket guide. It contains hundreds of helpful, practical tips to help get you started in the world of cutting-edge podcasting. If you're an entrepreneur and considering inbound marketing strategy - this is one of the best out there. Definitely give it a read!"

Nestene Botha

https://exploreprotech.com/

"With limited knowledge of the podcasting world, I am always mindful of differentiating between books that make for interesting reading and those that increase one's knowledge and provide a platform to apply the knowledge.

"Hendrik has successfully managed to incapsulate all three into one book, **Become a Podmaster**. It contains so much wisdom and expertise yet speaks a language that people like me can understand, allowing me to embrace rather than resist the benefits and value of podcasting and what it takes to Become a Podmaster.

"I now see podcasting through a different lens and recommend, if you are reading this, that you do the same.

"Thank you for sharing your expertise, your knowledge and wisdom, Hendrik."

Steven Levy

https://www.stevenlevy.co/

"In reading **How to Become a Podmaster**, I have picked up so many useful tips that can be applied not only to successful podcasts but video as well. I especially loved Hendrik's tip to speak to one and not all, as this is something I apply within my own business.

"The storytelling approach is very similar to how I focus on stories with my photography. It brings the audience into the story, the art, etc., and invites them to feel for that moment that they are experiencing it themselves. In **How to Become a Podmaster,** Hendrik explains how considering the listeners journey within the topic of your podcast episode is so important, and I agree!

"This is not only a book on podcasting, but also a quality business book. So much of the info within can be utilised in all aspects of running a successful business.

"If you are considering hosting a podcast or just starting out, then this is definitely a book to add to your collection. It will not only highlight what points are important but get you to think about areas you might not have considered, ending up with a podcast that grows your audience and meets the goals you had set out for it. Podcasts were not on my radar, but after reading this, I have a better understanding of them and may bring one into my own business at some point too.

"Thank you for sharing your knowledge and introducing me to a new opportunity to consider."

Joanne Moorhouse

https://brand.joannemoorhousephotography.com/links

"Having worked in podcasting for years, this book displays a thorough guide for both getting started with and growing your own show and even doing it for clients if you want to test the waters at consulting. Everything you need to think about and take action on is contained between these covers, making it the perfect resource for starting your digital business or for gifting to a friend in the industry. Take the time to go through this, do the exercises at the end of each chapter, and you will find yourself ahead of the game for sure."

Prenessa Nalliah

https://www.linkedin.com/in/prenessanalliah/

"Sage advice and recommendations clearly convey Hendrik's experience in this industry.

"This book is a recommended read for those curious about podcasting and all it entails. It's a fantastic guide for those serious about starting their journey as a podcaster. **Become a Podmaster** will become a bible of sorts - the amount of quality information shared is astounding!

"I appreciate Hendrik's 'warts-and-all' approach to sharing his expertise, which simultaneously serves as a reality check and a checklist. And I'm sure others will, too.

"Hendrik has put his heart into this one - his passion comes through strong."

Megan Deers

https://www.linkedin.com/in/megan-deers/

About the Author

Hendrik Baird studied Drama at the University of Pretoria, where he completed an honours degree. He has worked in the performance arts for the past 35+ years, most notably in developmental arts in the North-West Province of South Africa. Here he conceived and managed the North-West Cultural Calabash Arts Festival for many years.

He has at various times worked as an actor, magician, puppeteer, playwright, teacher, mentor, playwright, director, festival coordinator, and arts administrator, as well as appearing in feature films and television series, while also working behind the cameras from time to time.

Hendrik is a human rights activist. He a founding member of the non-profit Gay Umbrella and worked for OUT LGBT Well-Being, establishing a regional office in the North-West Province. He authored the report for the UNISA Centre of Applied Psychology research project conducted there in 2010.

Hendrik became a certified non-medical hypnotherapist in 2012 and regularly helps his clients to stop smoking and overcome their longstanding issues and problems. He had a very busy practice in Pretoria, but a heart attack in 2013 slowed him down for a while.

Hendrik has always liked to explore and learn new things, which led him to a media form he had not explore before, namely online radio. During his stint as station manager for GaySA Radio, he merged his arts skills and experience with that of his activism. Formatting the station from scratch was a huge challenge, and this is where Hendrik found out he could work well with his eldest son, Ethan, who was the station's Programming Manager.

During his time at the online radio, Hendrik spearheaded the successful campaign to have US hate-speech pastor Steven L. Anderson banned from entering South Africa. His work at GaySA Radio led to the station being nominated for a South African Radio Award and winning a Feather Award.

At the age of 57, Hendrik graduated with a master's degree in media and journalism in 2019. His research was into online radio. Since then he has pivoted to podcasting and, in 2021, started the company Baird Media (Pty) Ltd with his eldest son, Ethan Baird.

Hendrik is also the father of twins, Kyle and Caitlin. Kyle is an accomplished ballet dancer and Caitlin a professional barber. Their mother, Annemarie, is an actress and drama teacher.

Other Titles by Hendrik Baird

Same-Sex Sexuality in the North-West Province: Community Report on the Outcomes of a Research Project. (Unisa: Pretoria, 2010).

R@dio in South Africa: An Exploratory Study (with Franz Krüger). In *Radio, Public Life and Citizen Participation in South Africa,* edited by Sarah Chiumbu and Gilbert Motsaathebe. (Routledge: Oxon 2021).

Purposefully Repurposed for Profit: How to Save Time When Creating a Content Marketing Campaign Simply by Repurposing a Podcast. (Baird Media: Pretoria, 2022).

About Baird Media

At Baird Media, we produce content using a podcast-first approach. We help our clients use the power of podcasting to always be first in their customer's mind. Thereafter, we repurpose the podcast for the client's extended reach and engagement.

We strive to inspire business leaders to create high-quality, valuable, and useful content. Arrange a Virtual Coffee and let's have a chat about how you and your business can do this using podcasting as the source for content marketing campaigns.

Our team provides a variety of service, from scription, producing, editing, and packaging a podcast, to repurposing the podcast content for use as blogs, social media posts, and many others that will enrich the user experience and so grow audiences.

We are always keen to teach others who want to learn and consult with those who need help and advice. We consult individual clients on their specific needs and run small group training sessions, exploring the practical steps involved to start podcasting.

Look out for other books and blog articles that cover podcasting and content repurposing which are available on the website.

Should you need help with anything related to podcasting and content creation as explained in this book, or if you just want to talk about the topic and pick our brains, please contact us. You can find us at https://baird.media.

Ethan & Hendrik Baird

Thank you for buying this book. We would like to gift you the eBook version of **Purposefully Repurposed for Profit.**

Download it at
https://baird.media/free-book

Contents

Contents

Contents

Contents

Contents

Contents

Contents

"Podcasting is great. Total freedom."

—Bill Burr

Preface

Public speaking is a natural gift that comes easily to me and I have had to learn to adapt my speaking style to match the various audiences that have heard me speak. Among some of these challenges were: gauging audience responsiveness to my lectures under the darkened dome of the Johannesburg Planetarium; adapting to the discombobulating echo when addressing audiences in a large stadium; and learning to find effervescence when broadcasting to a huge unseen radio audience. When the opportunity came for me to script and present a weekly radio show, which the producers also released as a podcast, I thought I knew it all until I worked with Hendrik.

In no time at all, I realised that my podcasting knowledge was scant as I was under the misguided belief that podcasting simply meant reading my essay out loud and packaging the voice recording into a media file, which I could then quickly upload to the internet. How naïve I was.

Hendrik, with his vast pool of experience as an actor both on stage and on television, taught me so much more about podcasting. I already knew a bit about the importance of compelling content and the vital need to find spark in one's delivery, but I was a novice when it came to monetising one's podcast channel and utilising the opportunity to build networks. Furthermore, when Hendrik started teaching me about other podcasting benefits, I began to understand why the radio station not only needed me to produce a series of shows for broadcast but also wanted to release these episodes as a series of podcasts. These podcasts served to cleverly drive traffic back to their radio station and website, thereby building a stronger and better business.

One soon learns that radio and television are "hungry beasts." It can take days, weeks, or months to produce content for broadcast and once aired, the beast groans, belches and insatiably demands its next meal. Podcasting by contrast, builds up an archived pool of content that is forever accessible to a worldwide audience.

I was intrigued to learn from Hendrik that with a clever bit of forethought and planning, my show scripts could serve multiple other purposes. Like any aspirant podcaster, I soon realised that it is not enough to create a good podcast channel with compelling content in a niche market without driving traffic to it. Online advertising can be expensive and doesn't always achieve enough of a return on one's investment but by cleverly repurposing the same content, one is able to produce other content from what one already has, thereby growing one's network while saving a lot of time writing separate content for posting online.

No matter whether you are a budding enthusiast or corporate podcaster, I know that this book will improve the way you podcast.

Thomas Budge

https://startliving.co.za/

Introduction

It seems as if everyone wants to start a podcast. And who can blame them? Podcasting has grown rapidly over the past twenty years and, as with everything new, it is tempting to jump onto the bandwagon.

Few people who start out know what it takes to be a successful podcaster, and about two thirds of people give up before they reach episode 10. Podcast directories are littered with these failed attempts, and only a handful of people go on to make a success out of it.

Those who thought they would get rich from it are soon disillusioned, overwhelmed not only by the amount of work and technical skill it requires, but also because they cannot find the proverbial pot of gold at the end of the podcast rainbow.

Those who do achieve success do so either because they love the medium and pursue it as a hobby, or are shrewd entrepreneurs who understand what it takes to turn this medium into a profitable business.

This book is aimed at the new podcaster who is considering starting out in this medium but has no idea what it entails. At the same time, it targets the podcaster who has tried to produce podcast episodes but got lost and overwhelmed by it all. It will also provide valuable insights for the seasoned professional, delving deeper into aspects of the medium, highlighting aspects they may not have considered before.

This is not a step-by-step guide, yet I did my best to create a logical progression through all the aspects you need to take into consideration when starting a podcast for the first time. I have included actionable points, aimed at the new podcaster, to help shape and guide your planning, in an effort to keep you on track as you journey into this wonderful new media form. Each chapter ends with these Action Steps, suggesting the most pertinent actions to take towards producing your own podcast series.

As you will see, there is a great deal to consider before you start and much to accomplish as you begin the pre-production process. You will learn about the budgets required, the equipment you will need, and how to produce a podcast. Once the recording has been saved, the post-production process starts, including the all-important publishing and marketing steps, that ensure you get and grow an audience.

You will forgive me if I sometimes repeat myself, but there are certain things which are so important that I am compelled to repeat them, in the hope that it will sink in and make a lasting impression on you.

One of the words you will encounter repeatedly is "consistency." I cannot stress enough that if you decide that podcasting is for you, you must create a proper plan and consistently deliver on it. Another word you will encounter frequently as you work through this book, is "passionate." When you are passionate about podcasting and your topic, your chances of success increase tenfold.

In my own experience, podcasting is a fun activity through which you will learn a great deal about your chosen topic. You will get to speak to people you would not normally meet in your everyday life. And, at the end of the day, you will have the chance to share your message with the world.

More than that, you will be seen as a thought leader, as your audience gets to know and trust you.

It is my sincere wish that this book will open the world of podcasting for you and empower you to make it a success.

Hendrik Baird

Centurion, South Africa

23 November 2022

Part 1 - **production**

Chapter 1

Why Do **You** Want to Podcast?

"Podcasting is so frictionless from a creative point of view." —Taki Moore

Introduction

To say that podcasts are popular is the understatement of the century. This media form has grown rapidly during the past 20 years and the saturation point is still far in the future.

Before we look at why you want to start podcasting, it is important to understand why people are listening in the first place. As much as you want to communicate a certain message, it will be of no use if what you are trying to say does not resonate with your potential audience.

Podcasts are especially popular with the younger generation, specifically people under the age of 35. The older the person, the higher the likelihood of them listening to radio, which is the medium they grew up with. As the younger podcast listener demographic ages in the years to come, chances are they will continue listening to podcasts. Most of them do not even listen to or own a radio, so it is safe to say that the current younger audience will age with this media form.

The main reason they listen to podcasts is because they download episodes that cover topics that are of personal interest to them or because they want to learn something new. Some podcast listeners have time to kill and will listen to an episode or two to while away the time. Others will take a break from listening to music and choose a podcast as an alternative. Research has shown that Gen Z is more likely to look for entertainment or a change from music when choosing a podcast, while Gen Y is either looking to be entertained or want to fill empty time with something educational that keeps them updated.

The fact that one can multitask while listening to a podcast is a big plus. Sam is aged between 25-30 and resides in the United States. He says, "I think it's a bit more passive. You're able to multitask. Like, I can cook and listen to a podcast, for example." For Mar, aged between 31-35, also from the U.S., it is about control. He says, "With radio you can't control what shows are on, whereas with podcasts you can." Finally, there is Chloe, aged between 31-35, who is a U.K. citizen. According to her, "Podcasts are more of an outsider source of news or opinion, so you have a diverse range of news ideas and thoughts from vastly different people; not your traditional people who look and act a certain way" (Newman, 2019).

People start podcasting for distinct reasons. It is crucial that you have clarity exactly why you want to get started in this media form. Podcasts can educate, entertain, inform, inspire, get laughs, or make people cry. More importantly, they can connect. Podcasting is primarily an audio medium, which means there is a real human voice that conveys emotion through inflection and emphasis. The human voice is what gives life to the podcasts' content. It is also a portable medium, which means this content can go places other content has no access to. For this reason, it can connect in ways that other content cannot.

Video wants you to stop whatever you are doing and focus all your attention on it. Text demands your undivided attention and intelligence for you to make sense of what is written. Audio, on the other hand, moves with the listener as they navigate daily life. It does not demand every ounce of your attention, which is why you can listen to it while driving, preparing a meal, or exercising in the gym.

More than that, podcasts have the power to instantly connect with you on an entirely new and intimate level, no matter what they are trying to sell. And let's face it, we are all trying to sell something, whether it is an experience, information, a product or service, a story, an idea, or even yourself. Your audience will only buy what you have when they feel that they know, like, and trust you. This is where podcasting has the greatest power. What better way for a stranger to get to know you than when your voice vibrates in their heads through their earphones? Few things are as intimate as this.

Let us examine the reasons why you would want to start a podcast. Feel free to add your own reasons once you have worked through this list.

A Convenient Way to Consume Content

Marketing guru Seth Godin wrote, "Marketing is a contest for people's attention" (Cohen, 2021). In this modern world, we are constantly overwhelmed by all the information available at the click of a button. There is simply not enough time to concentrate fully on any one piece of content we want to consume, mostly because our attention spans are shorter than ever, and our focus divided. How can you focus all your attention on a video or written article when there are so many distractions around you?

The listen-through rate (LTR) for audio content is 59%. This means that more than half of the audience listen to the entire audio content. Compare this with the 15% view-through rate (VTR) of video and the 30% read rate (RR) of written content, and it will be clear that audio has the best chance of successfully communicating with your audience.

Ask any person to read a 500-page book and they will balk at the idea. Ask them to watch a 60-minute video on *YouTube* and very few will sit through even a quarter of it. Audio content is different in this regard. Long-form audio content has a three times higher engagement rate than short-form content. While there is no fixed rule as to how long a podcast should be, it seems that between 30-40 minutes hits the sweet spot, as it fits in with the time it takes to drive to work or do a workout at the gym.

Another interesting statistic is that people are very receptive to audio advertising, which scores a massive 91% LTR.

While you should still be producing written and video content, audio content will bring the its own unique results. This in and of itself should be good enough reason to consider starting a podcast.

It Is Inexpensive

You do not need many resources to start podcasting. Yes, if you have the budget, you can invest in fancy equipment and expensive studios, but this is not a prerequisite. Having an inexpensive microphone and a laptop, combined with a good set of headphones, together with recording and editing software (mostly free), are all you need to get going.

To start, you will want to be as self-contained as possible. You can expand your team down the line and outsource certain (or even all) of the tasks it takes to produce a podcast, but this is most certainly not necessary when you start out.

Publishing a podcast does not have to cost money in the beginning either. Most platforms have free packages to help you get started. You can always upgrade later and pay a small monthly hosting fee when you are up and running.

One of the remarkable things about a podcast is that you can record it wherever you are in the world. Recording while you are in a remote setting can add a new angle or flavour to your podcast, making you stand out from the crowd.

Easy to Produce

It does not take much to plan and record your first podcast episode. We will get into some more detail in a later chapter but suffice to say that all you need is an idea and a guest or two, and you will be on your way. Record the podcast and edit it using free software like *Audacity*. A *YouTube* video or two will teach you the basics if you have never edited audio before.

Once the podcast is edited, you simply upload it onto a host site and off you go! All you need to do now is to share the link with your friends and family and, before you know it, you will start getting downloads.

Great for Building Networks

One of the quickest ways of building a network is to interview guests for your show. People are usually very amenable to being interviewed, whether they are your family, friends, neighbours, or powerful executives of large companies.

There is something incredibly attractive about being interviewed for a podcast and you might find it easier than expected to get guests for your show. You will even be able to reach out to people that you might not have been able to reach otherwise. The bigger your audience, the easier it will be to get high profile experts to come onto your show.

Once you have interviewed somebody (and provided it went well) you will already have rapport with that person. This can result in every guest becoming a valuable contact in future. Regularly stay connected with your guests and chances are you will make new friends, establish partnerships for future projects, or share ideas that are to your mutual benefit. These people are also useful when it comes to sharing your podcast, so use this networking opportunity to your benefit.

Potential to Make Money

You can always just podcast as a hobby, but there are ways to monetize it, even if not immediately. If Joe Rogan could sign a multi-million deal with *Spotify*, you can too!

Of course, you will have to build up a massive audience before you would be considered for something like that, but in the meantime, there are other ways in which you could start making money off your podcast.

You can use your podcast as a platform to sell your products or services. If you have a book, courses, or consulting services, your podcast may be the ideal platform to promote them. In time you may consider getting a sponsor for your show or sell advertising, especially when your listener numbers have grown. You can also consider having affiliate links on your podcast website, recommending products to your listeners, earning commission from any sales that are made through your links.

In time, as you position yourself as a thought leader, you may charge people a fee to appear on your show, especially if they are from large companies who want to showcase their own services or products. You may even consider making episodes on-demand for a fee, for others to use on their websites or in their marketing campaigns.

Position Yourself as An Authority

Let us suppose you know quite a bit about a specific topic, such as gardening. When you use your podcast to share helpful gardening tips on a consistent basis, you will position yourself as a gardening authority. Just like when you regularly write blog articles or have authored a book on the subject, a podcast will help develop your reputation as an expert in your field.

The advantage of doing this is that you may start to get invitations to speak at events or conferences, or people may make use of your consulting services, or even buy products from you.

The difference between somebody who knows much about a specific industry and a thought leader, is that a thought leader publishes content. Once you put your ideas and thoughts in the public domain, you will be perceived as someone who stands out above the rest, deserving of respect and prestige. Soon you will be able to facilitate thought provoking conversations through your podcast and you will be putting yourself in the epicentre of your field or industry. This is more than what 99% of others in your industry are doing, which means you will be seen as an authority in your field.

It is not uncommon for people who start podcasting to experience the "imposter syndrome," meaning they feel out of place and undeserving of their achievements. This may be the case as you produce your first batch of podcast episodes, but things will start to change as you get into the rhythm of producing a regular stream of episodes. By episode 20 you will become more comfortable in this space and your interview techniques will have improved, as you get to know the medium better. Soon, you will start attracting well-known people onto your show.

Before you know it, others in your industry will start reaching out to you and you will receive pitches from people and companies who want to be featured on your show. You may even be seen as an influencer, like Diana Chen of the *Startup Happy Hour Podcast*. Ms. Chen started her career as an attorney and turned to podcasting when she wanted to make a career move into the start-up industry.

Her podcast had been going for barely six months when she was approached by the founders of start-ups who wanted to be featured on her show. Her guests were credible and fitted into the personas of those she wanted to interview and network with. It wasn't long before she was appointed in the position of Head of Content Marketing at a start-up with a six-figure salary. She had moved from an entry level person to being an influencer, changing her career trajectory and how she was perceived in the start-up industry. It just goes to show that when you are perceived as a thought leader, it can have a positive impact on your career and business.

Opportunities to Repurpose Content

There are two ways to repurpose your content using a podcast. If you have already produced blog articles or video content, you can easily turn these into a podcast. You may simply read your written content and record it as podcast episodes. In this way, your written content gets a new lease on life by being exposed to a new audience.

Audio can be extracted from video and presented in podcast format, although care must be taken that it is edited in such a way that it makes sense without the visuals.

A podcast can also be the source material for other forms of content. Once you have recorded a podcast episode, you can have it transcribed, giving you a word-for-word written version. You may then decide to write a blog article or two based on the podcast. You may even produce infographics or other visual content based on the most pertinent points of the podcast.

Consider also turning the audio podcast into a *YouTube* video, either by recording the interview on a platform like *Zoom*, or by adding graphics to the audio. There are people who choose to consume their podcasts in video format, so make sure you utilize this opportunity to reach a wider audience.

Increase Traffic to Your Website

To consistently drive traffic to your website, you need content that is valued as entertaining, insightful, and useful to the audience. The importance of producing podcast episodes regularly cannot be stressed enough for this to work. Your audience must want to come back to your website often to listen to the latest episode. This means that you will need a clear marketing strategy for your podcast that will get people to subscribe.

Your podcast will need to have a strong personality that your audience finds relatable. It must be unique, so that they will come back repeatedly, as they are unable to find the same content somewhere else. How you brand your podcast will have a key role to play here. It may take time before you find your unique voice and hone in on the content that your audience relates to the most, therefore a testing phase is always recommended.

You will need to use social media to drive traffic to your website and having a good podcast will make it much easier to leverage your social media channels in that regard. Making use of quotes extracted from the podcast, or using video or audio snippets, will create intrigue and interest, while free downloads attached to each episode can add value.

Summary

It does not matter if you want to podcast for fun or for profit, just make sure that your reasons for starting are solid. When you consider that more than a quarter of all podcasts only have one episode, while 64% have less than 10 episodes, it should be clear that not having a good enough motivation will see your efforts come to naught within a short space of time. Consistently creating good podcast episodes at regular intervals requires commitment and sustained effort on your part. Make sure the reasons you venture into this field are solid and the benefits tangible.

Do not start if you are only fascinated by the outcome but underestimate the amount of work it will require to produce regular episodes. Do not start podcasting if you think you should have one because everyone else is doing it. You will not make quick money, nor will it take only 10 or 20 minutes of your time every week. If you are not prepared to promote your podcast, it will be a waste of your time and energy. If you just want to emulate another podcast and do not have any original ideas of your own, stop right now, as you will not succeed.

Without at least the basic equipment, you will not get far.

Worse still, if you have never listened to a podcast before, do not start producing one. You will need to listen to as many podcasts as you can before you even consider setting up your first interview. Like everything, research is important, otherwise how will you know what the standards are, what entertains you and what doesn't, what works and what fails?

There is nothing worse than a dead podcast, one which started but went nowhere. The field is littered with such corpses. Ensure that your motivation for starting one is strong enough to sustain you in the long term. Do it for the right reasons and success is sure to follow.

Action Steps

✓ Do you have any ideas for a podcast? Write down your areas of expertise and determine if there is enough material for a podcast series. Evaluate your ideas and find the one that excites you the most.

✓ Once you have decided on one or more, flesh out the ideas and see how it can be structured to tell a story. What is that story? How best will you tell it?

✓ Who is the ideal person who would listen to your podcast?

✓ What benefit will they get from listening to your podcast?

Chapter 2

Who is Your Ideal Listener?

"I'd tell anyone who wants to be a podcaster, the same thing others have recommended – find a niche you're passionate about and willing to be immersed in." —Sandra Sealy

Introduction

There are too many people who start their podcast by saying, "Hello everybody!" or "Hey guys!" This is a crucial mistake that newcomers make. Not everybody is going to listen to your podcast. There isn't a hall full of people anxiously waiting to listen to your podcast as if they were in a theatre waiting for a performance to start.

The moment you abstract your listener in this way by lumping them into a nebulous group, is the moment you create distance between yourself and them. People are far less likely to respond to any calls to action when they are addressed as a group instead of as an individual. The reason for this is that they are not hearing the ask on a subconscious level and may feel that there is nothing they personally must do.

Your podcast audience consists of only one person. You should always only speak to that one, solitary person. They are probably wearing earphones and listening in private while doing something else. You are going to have to be clear from the start who that person is to whom you are talking.

This means you will have to understand how old they are, what race, sex, and gender they are, what income group they fall into, and what they are doing while listening to your podcast (which will give you an indication of how long it should be). The more specific you are about your listener avatar, the more specifically you can gear your show to that one person.

Your ideal listener should have a name, a backstory, and even a picture you prominently display while you record your podcast, as if you are talking to that person and that person alone. You should know where they live, what kind of work they do, as well as having insights into their family life.

It is only once you have a clear idea of who your ideal listener is, that you will be able to create content that appeals to them. Think of your podcast as a story. To best tell your story, you need to know who it is that you are telling your story to. Telling a story to a child is different to the way you would to a teenager, a mother, or a grandfather. Your approach to storytelling will be different when you are relating it to a filmmaker as opposed to a world traveller.

The duration of your podcast episodes will depend in large part on who you are targeting. A stay-at-home mother may only have a precious few minutes to spare between changing nappies and doing the laundry, while a long-distance commuter may have more time to sit back and listen.

How will you know where to target potential listeners in your marketing campaign if you have no idea who the podcast is for? Do they spend time on social media and, if so, which channels? The more detailed your listener avatar is, the more specifically you can target them. The more you know about their daily habits, the easier it will be to create content that engages them.

When your podcast speaks to one person at a time, the listener will feel connected. By constantly referring to that one listener, they start to feel valued and appreciated. This makes it even more likely that they will buy into your podcast and whatever you are offering in your call to action.

Take the time to define your ideal listener in as much detail as you can and use it as a constant reference point during your podcast. The results may just astound you.

Create Your Ideal Listener Avatar

If you are in business, the idea of creating a customer avatar may not be a foreign concept to you. You may have already done this exercise to determine your ideal customer. The same must be done for your podcast, so that you can be certain exactly to whom you are speaking. The avatar is a persona that represents a listener that you already have or that you want to have, or even one that you want to avoid.

The more detailed and specific you are when compiling this avatar, the more accurately you can target your podcast to that person. You may create more than one persona if you feel it will be helpful. Less than half of podcasters do this exercise before they start, so gain the advantage over your competition by taking the time to be as detailed as possible with the persona.

You may wonder if you are not alienating the listeners who do not fit the persona you have created. Of course, they will still get the message and they may respond to your call to action. However, your ideal listener will find your content even more appealing and will be more likely to buy whatever it is you are selling.

A negative persona is the opposite of your ideal listener. These are the people that will never listen to your podcast or respond to your calls to action. Whatever you are offering will not appeal to them or fit into their lifestyle. Compiling this persona in addition to that of your ideal listener is useful, as it will help you to avoid them. You obviously do not want to waste any advertising spend on people who will never buy from you, either because they are not interested in what you have to offer or because they do not have the disposable income to do so.

You also do not want bad reviews or negative comments, so protect your reputation by getting consistently complimentary reviews and comments from your ideal listeners and avoid those who may run you down simply because they are not your ideal audience.

Determine the Listener Demographics

Ideally, you want to build your ideal listener avatar by answering the following questions.

➤ What is the name of your ideal listener?

➤ What is their gender?

➤ What is their marital status?

➤ What does their family look like?

➤ What level of education do they have?

➤ What type of job do they have?

➤ How much do they earn monthly?

➤ How do they spend their monthly budget?

➤ Where do they usually shop?

➤ Who makes the purchasing decisions?

➤ What motivates the decision-maker to make a purchase?

➤ Where does the decision-maker go when they need advice?

➤ Where do they stay?

➤ What kind of car do they drive?

➤ What is their daily routine?

➤ What magazines and newspapers do they read?

➤ What are their favourite social media channels?

➤ What TV shows do they watch?

➤ Which streaming services are they subscribed to?

➤ What podcasts do they listen to?

➤ What are they doing while listening to podcasts?

➤ How much time do they spend listening to podcasts every week/month?

➤ What time of the day do they usually listen to podcasts?

➤ Who do they vote for?

➤ Who are their heroes?

➤ Who do they despise?

➤ What social issues move them the most?

➤ What social issues do they not care about?

➤ What is their greatest want?

- ➤ What is their greatest need?
- ➤ What is their greatest fear?
- ➤ What does their business look like?
- ➤ What hobbies do they have?
- ➤ Where do they go on holiday?
- ➤ How do they prefer to communicate?

What Are Your Listener's Pain Points?

Every one of us have a specific problem that we need to address. This is what is referred to as a pain point. These can be varied and diverse, depending on the person themself and the situation(s) they find themself in.

Your ideal listener may not be aware that they have a pain point but finding out what it is will help you to shape your podcast. This will help them not only realize their problem, but also see the value in your product or service that provides the solution they need to resolve whatever their problem might be.

Pain points can broadly be grouped into four categories.

- ✓ **Process pain points.** When someone experiences problems concerning internal processes, they are inefficient and unproductive. They are in effect trying to accomplish something but not achieving it because of outdated or inefficient ways of thinking or doing.

- ✓ **Productivity pain points.** This type of pain point is associated with process pain points. It occurs when people are not using their time effectively by for instance spending too much time on a certain task.

- ✓ **Financial pain points.** A person experiencing this pain point is either spending far too much money and wants to reduce their spending, or does not have access to adequate finances to begin with.

- ✓ **Support pain points.** A person who experiences support pain points has issues finding help when they most need it.

When you can start identifying which pain points dominate for your ideal listener, your podcast can start answering the questions they have and provide workable solutions. Note that these pain points can be business related, such as when a customer has problems getting support when they are on their buying journey, or it can be personal in nature, such as when a person does not know who to turn to for support when experiencing depression or anxiety.

The root causes of the pain points may be as diverse as the people who experience them. To unearth them, you will need to embark on qualitative research that focuses on open-ended questions through which you will be able to get individualized and detailed responses. You may need to interview people in real life who fit into the ideal listener persona you have created. The research results could function as a handy guide to help you find the right theme and subsequent content for your podcast.

What Is Your Niche?

You can only start to plan your podcast once you have a thorough understanding of who your ideal listener is. One of the main reasons why podcasts fail is because it does not cater to a specific type of listener.

It is so easy to just start recording something you are passionate about, or think is interesting, but unless you have taken the time to create a detailed listener avatar, your chances of success are slim. One of the most common mistakes people new to podcasting make, is to underestimate the importance of this first step. If you have no idea who the podcast is aimed at, listeners will not magically appear after working out for themselves that it is indeed suitable for them. Having the avatar will influence everything from this point forward.

Nobody wants to waste their precious time searching through millions of podcasts to find the right ones for them. They want to listen to content that fits their interests, no matter how niched those interests might be. It is only when you are clear about exactly who you are aiming your content at, that it will become focused and relevant. You will be well advised to choose a niche that fits the ideal listener you have defined.

"A podcast niche is a narrowly defined topic that interests a specific audience" (Castos, 2021). How do you know what your niche is? You look at your ideal listener and consider other people that are similar, finding the things they have in common and then focusing on the specifics. It might be helpful to think of a niche as a subcategory. Your ideal listener might be someone who has just given birth and who is struggling with postpartum depression. Your main category may be "new moms," but your subcategory should be "ways of dealing with postpartum depression."

A niche helps to narrow the scope of the topic. The deeper you can niche into your niche, the more specific the content of your podcast will become. Choosing topics that are of general interest may work for celebrities who have large followings, but you will only start to stand out when you really drill down into your niche. The more you niche down, the better the chances that what you will be presenting will be unique.

Podcast Professor Lij Shaw says it best, "By trying to market to everyone out there, you'll end up marketing to no one at all, because you simply won't reach anyone through all the noise on the internet" (Shaw, 2015). You might think that drilling down into your niche will exclude people, and you would be right. This is not a bad thing. It will be to your advantage to drill down as deeply into your niche as you can to target a specific audience. Doing so will expand your audience base instead of limiting it.

Let us go back to the topic of postpartum depression (PPD). While it is true that this issue affects women, did you know that 25% of men are seriously affected by PPD too? It presents as social withdrawal, distractions at work, feeling unmotivated, changes in sleep, appetite, and weight, and even alcohol and substance abuse, amongst other symptoms? Let us say you choose to drill down into just one of these symptoms as your niche, it allows your podcast to become laser focused. It also means that you may have to redo your ideal listener avatar to fit into the niche that you have discovered.

How to Choose Your Podcast Niche

Choosing your niche is your decision, provided your choice is based on the ideal listener avatar and in-depth research. How exactly you will determine your niche is therefore up to you, but you may want to follow these steps to help you find your way.

Begin with a general list. Start by writing down your ideas. Do not censor yourself here, write down as many ideas as you can, even if they sound silly.

It does not matter if the ideas are niched enough or even marketable, this is not important at this point of the exercise. You will start narrowing it down soon enough.

Use these questions to help you produce ideas:

- ✓ Which topics are you most well-informed about?

- ✓ Which activities or hobbies do you like doing?

- ✓ What are the things that you are passionate about?

- ✓ What are the things that excite you?

- ✓ What are the things people ask your advice about?

- ✓ What are the things people consider you to be an expert in?

You may want to browse through some podcast titles to stimulate your ideas.

Consider the subjects you love. There is no point starting a podcast and not enjoy doing it. Choosing subjects that you love and genuinely enjoy will help you during those times when creating yet another podcast episode will seem like arduous work. Make no mistake, producing a regular podcast is demanding and podfading is a real thing. You may start strong but lose motivation as time goes by and your podcast will fade into obscurity as you miss publishing deadlines. Consistency is the key to a successful podcast. You will have a much bigger chance of remaining consistent when the subject you cover is at least something you really enjoy.

At the same time, think of the subjects your ideal listener will enjoy. There is no point in having a podcast that only you enjoy, is there? You need other people to find the topic as engaging as you do, so that you can build an audience.

- ✓ **What makes you different?** You will surely stand out when your podcast offers something that cannot be found elsewhere. Being different will make your podcast competitive and will give people a reason to listen to it. You may write down unique experiences you have had or interesting stories that give you a special perspective. You may have a certain expertise that can be applied in an unusual way, or you may know genuinely interesting people that can be your guests.

✓ **What are your strengths and expertise?** It will be a good idea to choose a topic that you understand well. It will be so much easier talking about something you know much about than trying to first learn about a topic you know nothing about. You may not know everything about your topic and research may be required, but starting from a position of power will give you the edge.

✓ **What is relevant in the world today?** When you are informed of current affairs, you will be able to identify topics that people are talking about or want to know more of. As much as you want your podcast to be relevant to the time you are producing it, you should also consider keeping the topics evergreen. This means that it must still be relevant in years to come. When your topics are anchored around specific events, such as Black Friday specials, it will have a limited shelf life and a narrow audience. Find ways to open up specific or seasonal events in a way that will make the podcast relevant in times to come.

✓ **What is your competition doing?** Once you start to understand your niche and the topics that may interest your ideal listener, do research into what the competition is doing, specifically those podcasts that appeal to you. Who are these podcasters and what show formats are they using? Why are they popular? You will soon see that there are certain topics, like true crime, weight loss, or comedy, which have saturated the market. It might be difficult (but not impossible) to establish yourself in those categories. Do not be afraid of competition, it is a good thing. Seeing categories that are similar to your chosen niche is a positive sign, as it means there is already an audience for it.

✓ **How far can you drill down into the subcategories?** You do not want to compete with the big players such as celebrities and media studios that have large budgets. This will limit your potential growth and have the opposite effect of you standing out from the crowd. Remember, just because you have chosen a niche does not mean you are imprisoned by it. You can always narrow it down or expand it as time goes by and as you learn more about your audience and what they like. Podcasters often adjust their topic during the first year, when they start getting feedback from their fans. You have to start somewhere, so focus on one aspect of a broader topic.

✓ Do not be scared of asking others their opinion. If you have friends, arrange small focus groups, chat through your ideas, and get their feedback. If you have a co-host, involve them in the process, as you must be comfortable with a niche that suits you both. Write things down, compare notes, make compromises where necessary, and do whatever you need to find a topic you both enjoy.

✓ **Will you be able to monetize it?** Most people start a podcast with the aim of earning money from it. This should not be your first consideration when starting out but do take it into account when choosing your niche. There are diverse ways you could make money off your podcast, and they will be dealt with in detail later. You are going to have to consider whether your potential niches have the potential of attracting money in one way or another. It is encouraging to know that "niche podcasts with a small but engaged audience have the potential to be the biggest money-making audio shows for publishers" (Tobitt, 2022).

Your niche matters because it will give direction to your content, in the same way as a business plan gives direction to how a company is operated. Only once you have determined your niche, can you start developing themes, outlines, and individual episodes.

Having a niche will differentiate you from the rest and create a brand. The more unique you are, the more you will stand out. This will reduce the amount of competition you have. It may narrow down your potential audience, but as it also narrows down your competition, you will have a better chance to really connect with your ideal listener. This has the potential to translate into a loyal following.

Once you have brainstormed the possibilities and looked at your competition, you need to conduct your market research. Go back to your ideal listener avatar and redo it if you need to. Do your research about your ideal listener, so that you can really determine what they want to listen to, that they cannot find somewhere else.

You will soon have a loose idea of where you want to go, and which niche you want to target. This is the time to start experimenting with outlines. Write down ideas for each of the episodes for at least the first six months of the show. It will help you determine a flow and progression as you explore aspects of your topic in each episode. This can later be developed into the season plan.

Summary

Determining your ideal listener is the first key step to complete before you even think about recording your first episode. The more specific you are, the better your chances of success. Do not create just one avatar, do at least three. Once you have determined your niche, return to the avatar and fine tune it, or even redo it completely.

The ideal listener and your niche will impact everything you do from this point forward. Revisit it from time to time, just as you may revisit a business plan as your business grows and develops.

Podcasting is the most intimate form of interaction across all modern media platforms, as it is consumed by a person listening with earphones. You will be communicating directly into their heads, a sacred space to say the least. They will get to know your tastes, tics, the phrases you use, indeed your whole personality from your voice alone. They will start feeling close to you and begin to trust you. They will be able to tell immediately whether you are genuine and authentic or not.

Your goal is to establish a connection with your listener. The more specific you are about who you are talking to and what interests them the most, the more successful your podcast will end up being. More than half of consumers in the 21st century will remain loyal to brands that "get them" or understand them on a deeper, personal level (Saraswati, 2022). They will start consuming your content more frequently and start recommending you.

Unlock your listener's trust, loyalty, and intimacy, by doing them the honour of understanding them on the deepest level possible. Success is sure to follow.

Action Steps

✓ Compile three or more avatars to represent your ideal listener and at least one representing those you do not want as listeners.

✓ Start looking at the niches you can cover in your podcast. Make lists of sub-niches and see how far you can drill down. Which topics do you find that are of interest to you?

✓ Can you connect the ideal listener with the niche?

Chapter 3

Podcast Genres and Formats

"I like the freedom of podcasting. With podcasting you can really mess around with the form and the format. You can do as much time as you like without having to pause for commercials." —Adam Carolla

Introduction

At this point, you should have a clear idea of who your podcast is aimed at and what niche it falls into. The next step is to decide on the format and genre that will make your podcast unique. You need to determine these even before choosing a name for your podcast or designing any cover artwork.

The genre and format will depend heavily on the type of content your audience wants to listen to. They will be looking for consistency, knowing what to expect. You also want to have consistency in the way you produce your podcast, so that you do not have to begin from scratch every time. Having a clearly defined genre and format allows you to design a template that you can use every time you structure your episodes.

Different formats are suitable for different types of content. Some are quite easy to produce, while others may take more time and effort. The more you know about what options are available to you, the easier your job will become overall.

What Are Genres and Formats?

Genres

The genre is the category your podcast will fall into. It is the theme of the podcast that will determine the topics that are discussed. As podcast audiences continue to grow, it is becoming clear that certain genres are more popular than others. Music, television and movies, comedy, technology, and kids and family, lead the pack.

The fanbase for these genres can be broken down into avid and casual fans.

The avid fans are the ones who see themselves as extremely interested in a certain genre. This is obviously the kind of listener you want to attract to your podcast, as they will download episodes week after week, religiously following the podcasts they subscribe to. Other genres that have a high number of avid fans are games and hobbies, sports, and technology.

Casual fans are more laid back. They enjoy their chosen genres, know a bit of trivia, and enjoy what they choose to listen to. They are not as fanatic as avid fans, who will have in-depth knowledge, such as the sports buff who can quote game statistics and name players.

Genre List

Here is a detailed genre list with sub-genres. This list is by no means complete, as new genres are being created all the time. If you get stuck for genre ideas, visit your local library, and browse through all the various categories on the shelves. You are bound to get inspired by the ideas you will find there.

- ➤ Advice & Self-help.
- ➤ Arts: Books, Design, Fashion & Beauty, Food, Performing Arts, Visual Art.
- ➤ Audio Dramas.
- ➤ Business: Careers, Entrepreneurship, Finance, Investing, Management, Marketing, Non-Profit, Real Estate.
- ➤ Comedy: Comedy Interviews, Improv, Stand-Up.

- Education: Courses, How To, Language Learning, Self-Improvement.
- Environment & Science.
- Feminist.
- Fiction: Comedy Fiction, Drama, Romance, Science Fiction.
- Food & Drinks.
- Games & Hobbies.
- Game Show.
- Government.
- Health & Fitness: Alternative Health, Fitness, Medicine, Mental Health,
- Nutrition, Self-Help, Sexuality.
- History.
- Interview Cast.
- Investigative Journalism.
- Kids & Families: Education for Kids, Family, Parenting, Pets & Animals, Stories for Kids.
- Law.
- Leisure: Animation & Manga, Automotive, Aviation, Crafts, Games, Hobbies, Home & Garden, Video Games.
- Music: Music Commentary, Music History, Music Interviews.
- News: Business News, Daily News, Entertainment News, News Commentary, Politics, Sports News, Tech News.
- Politics.
- Philosophy.
- Pop Culture.
- Religion & Spirituality: Buddhism, Christianity, Hinduism, Islam, Judaism, Religion, Spirituality.
- Reviews.
- Science: Astronomy, Chemistry, Earth Sciences, Life Sciences, Mathematics, Natural Sciences, Nature, Physics, Social Sciences.
- Society & Culture: Documentary, Personal Journals, Philosophy, Places & Travel, Relationship.

➤ Sports: Baseball, Basketball, Cricket, Fantasy Sports, Football, Golf, Hockey, Rugby, Running, Soccer, Swimming, Tennis, Volleyball, Wilderness, Wrestling.

➤ Technology.

➤ Travel.

➤ True Crime.

➤ TV & Film: After Shows, Film History, Film Interviews, Film Reviews, TV Reviews.

How To Choose a Genre

We are all different and we have varied interests. It will be helpful to examine the reason you want to podcast and then make a list of your skills and interests. Whether you are going to podcast as a hobby or promote your business, will play a key role in deciding which genre is best suited to your podcast. The genre you choose will have an influence on your niche, which of course will make you stand out from the crowd.

When deciding on your genre, pick a subject that you love and are passionate about. Consider the things you genuinely enjoy. Making a podcast will take effort and time, so why would you select something you have no interest in? You will have more fun with a topic that you enjoy. There will be a temptation to pick one of the most popular genres, but only do so if you have a specific affinity with the subject matter. There will be fierce competition in the most popular genres, which means you will get lost in the noise, unless you have a standout idea and superior knowledge and expertise in that specific field.

You may have an interest in more than one genre. Narrow your choices down by deciding what your strengths are. What did you study? What work experience do you have? Which hobbies or activities do you excel at? Which topics do you want to learn more about? It will be easier to research something that you already are familiar with, and you will certainly enjoy finding out more about it.

Consider which topics your ideal listener will enjoy the most. Podcasts are not only about you, but also about your listener. You might want to do research among people who look like your ideal listener to find out what they enjoy listening to or what they want to know more about. If you intend to start a business podcast, for instance, find out what the customers' pain points are and gear your podcast toward providing them with practical solutions that your business service or products can provide.

The most popular genres might be a tempting choice, but the competition will be fierce. If you decide to enter a popular genre, find a unique angle, such as focusing on unsolved crimes in the true crime genre, instead of just looking at interesting crime cases. What will set you apart from your competition is your unique perspective on the genre. This will only become clear once you have done a thorough investigation of the competition, so that you can find the gaps that are not covered. This will help you to sharpen your niche.

Your podcast will hopefully continue regularly into the future. While you want to start by having a narrow focus, you must also consider how you can broaden your topic in future when you run out of content. You will want to keep your audience excited and engaged during every episode, so reflect on ideas that can diversify the focus in future.

Your podcast genre will play a defining role in your niche, so make sure you start on a strong footing and increase the chances of success by taking your time to find the right genre for you.

Formats

Whereas the genre is the "what" of your podcast, the format defines the "how." There are at least eleven formats, some more popular than others. Formats can be mixed and matched, making clear definitions tricky, but for the sake of clarity the main formats will be explained here. You are welcome to get creative and create a format that suits your genre and niche more specifically.

Solo Podcast

Also known as the monologue podcast, this format consists of the podcast host speaking alone throughout each episode. This is a common and popular format and especially suitable for the host who is an expert in their subject.

As the name suggests, this format involves just one person delivering the content.

Recording this type of podcast is easier than any of the rest. It is easy to edit, as you just have to take out your fluffs and stutters, add the opening and closing billboards, and you are on your way. This format requires considerable skill from the host. They must come across as being enthusiastic and full of energy. This may not be so easy for the novice.

This type of podcast is usually scripted but it should not come across as someone reading a script. People who listen to podcasts do not want to hear somebody reading; instead, they want someone who speaks engagingly.

This format works well in several genres, such as commentary, fiction, non-fiction, and question-and-answer sessions. In fact, it can be applied to any topic, if you have the relevant experience and expertise. A fair amount of research is still required to add value for the listener. To make this format a success, you must keep up your enthusiasm, smile when you record your script, and be as engaging as you can.

Co-Hosted (Conversational) Podcast

A podcast with two hosts is also quite popular and a little easier to produce, as it does not only depend on one person to carry the whole show. This format works best when you have somebody who is as enthusiastic about your topic as you are and with whom you already have rapport. The opportunity to have fun while recording this type of podcast is high, especially if there is chemistry between the hosts.

The co-hosted podcast has room for fun banter, opposing or differing viewpoints, and deeper insights, if both hosts are well-informed about the topic under discussion. It also helps to share the research and presenting workload, making it a great format.

The presenting style should be conversational, like the traditional radio show. Be warned though, this format will test your improvisational skills. You will have to think quickly and ad lib your way through unscripted moments.

A guest may sometimes be included in this format. The secret to success is however the familiarity between the hosts. Imagine presenting a show with somebody you barely know or that you do not have a good relationship with!

The two hosts can be in the same room or studio when recording, but could also be in separate locations, connecting online, which may present its own challenges that will need to be overcome.

Interview Podcast

This format has a host or two who speak with one or more guests in each episode. The guest is usually an expert in their subject, theme, or industry. This format also lends itself to interacting with people you would not normally meet, such as celebrities or high-profile businesspeople, making it an excellent networking tool.

The interview can cover one topic specifically or can be an opportunity to elicit people's opinions about assorted topics. Most importantly, the host must have excellent listening skills and be able to ask follow-up questions to explore interesting side-avenues the conversation might veer into.

Inexperienced hosts usually make the mistake of using the interview as an excuse to air their own opinions, sometimes not even giving the guest enough time to speak. A good host is worth their weight in gold and, if done well, this type of podcast can become exceedingly popular with its target audience.

There are two approaches that can be taken with this format. The first is to interview experts where the interviewee is approached as a thought leader. The ideal listener would listen to this type of podcast because they want to learn something about a specific industry or field, gaining fresh insights that will be of benefit to them.

Entertainment interviews involve sharing interesting stories or experiences about the guests' lives. Interviewing actors is an example of this, where they will chat about their experiences, roles, and (if you're lucky) their private lives.

A certain level of research is required to get the best content out of the interviewee. The skilled host will get the guest to relax sufficiently to relate interesting stories about themselves. This format is also a fantastic way to highlight different viewpoints and opinions.

Panel Podcasts

A roundtable podcast, consisting of a panel, can talk about almost every topic under the sun. This format works particularly well when the panellists are passionate about the subject matter. It is also a popular format among podcast audiences. Getting the right mix of panellists may be tricky, as you will want the banter and dynamics to be entertaining yet informative.

Coordinating this type of show may be complicated, as you will have to synchronize the schedules of the participants. You may also have to manage the different personalities, avoiding potential problems and conflicts. The show can consist of the same panel for every episode, or the panel can rotate, with a central host to keep continuity.

The best panel podcasts consist of a group, each of whom have a particular strong point. One may be the expert, another the joker, and a third may be the one asking the questions. Panel shows with the same members become like a private club and regular listeners will notice in-jokes and personality quirks, which in and of itself can be very entertaining.

Non-Fiction Narrative Storytelling

Often, you will find this format in the true crime genre, although it is such a popular format that you can almost say it is a genre on its own. It takes the form of an audio documentary, unravelling a story or event from real life over one or more episodes. It is ideally suited to the podcaster who likes solving mysteries or who likes telling true tales that are unusual or gripping in nature.

Of all the formats, the investigative podcast will most probably need the most research and resources. It will also require a superior level of editing skill to tell the story in an engaging, suspenseful, and entertaining manner. Get it right and you will soon have avid fans who will quickly spread the word to their circle of influence.

Podcast Theatre

This format is also known as Fictional Storytelling. It is like a fiction series on television, where the story is usually told in serial form over multiple episodes. These kinds of podcasts will need a cast of voice actors and a crew to produce. It will have sound effects and musical elements to add to the tension of the story, as well as to the climaxes and cliff-hangers.

Podcast theatre is perfect for creative storytellers who know how to use the power of audio to tell a story. Fiction writers and film directors might find it a creative way to express themselves. Podcast theatre is different from having a book read online like an audiobook. Podcast theatre has more creative elements to it, such as character, plots, and themes.

Repurposed Content Podcasts

Let us suppose you have authored articles for your blog. You can repurpose these blogs into podcasts and so get extra value from its transformation. There is much content that can be repurposed into podcasts. Extract the audio from video and re-edit it; record your lectures and release them as podcasts; record the weekly religious sermon and turn it into a downloadable podcast; a comedian recording his stand-up routines has enough material to produce a regular podcast.

Video Podcast

Video podcasting or vidcasting is becoming increasingly popular. Adding a camera to your podcast recording has become a necessity, enabling you to reach large audiences through video platforms such as *YouTube*. It can be as simple as a static camera focused on the host and guest, or it can be a multi-camera production. You can insert clips to make it more dynamic, such as news or other soundbites.

Zoom meetings have in recent times become a way for people from around the globe to interact. While the sound quality of such a call may not always be of a studio standard, it can be corrected by recording each speaker individually, giving more editing and sound control options during the sound processing and mastering steps. One could also use proper audio equipment on either end of a remote call, record it separately, and edit it all together later.

Improv Podcasts

Those who have been blessed by a razor-sharp wit and who can improvise on the spot, often to hilarious effect, should consider Improv Podcasts. This format can feature one or more hosts or even full casts, where everything is improvised or ad libbed. There might sometimes be a broad script or guide, or it might follow a theme or specific topic.

Improv podcasting is quite versatile, as it can be used in several niches. Game shows thrive on improv, as do comedic routines, monologues, and fictional storytelling. Do not mistake improv for being unprepared. When you are unprepared, it will always show. When you can improvise by thinking on your feet, you can create magic.

Tabletop Podcasts

This is a very niched format aimed at the tabletop role-playing gamers. There are gamers who record themselves playing games like *Dungeons and Dragons.* These actual play podcasts combine the excitement of being "on-air" with the banter of a panel podcast, to which is added the game's storytelling aspect with its intrigue and excitement.

This podcast is also used to share information with inexperienced players by having expert table-top game players on the show. Many unpractised players have been introduced to these types of games through this podcast format and its success begs to be repeated within another niche.

Hybrid Podcasts

Podcasting is such a new media form that we should at this stage reserve space for innovation. We should all be free to experiment, mix and match formats, while inventing our own, as we get to know the medium better.

No matter the theme or format of your podcast, the result should be entertaining. It is not worth doing if it does not entertain. It cannot add value if it is boring, because then nobody will listen to it. The message will only stand out when the podcast is engaging and makes you feel something. Feel free to play around with formats once you have mastered the basics.

Live or Pre-recorded?

There is a certain allure to sitting in a studio and broadcasting live into the ether, hopefully to listeners at the other end. This is what made radio so successful, surviving death threats by video stars and others. In podcasting, there is a case to be made for both live and pre-recorded, and even a hybrid of the two. To understand the pros and cons of each more clearly, let us briefly look at radio first.

Radio usually has a set schedule that must be adhered to. Listeners will tune in and out of a radio broadcast, therefore the need to continually reintroduce the show, host, and station, as well as to remind listeners what topic is being talked about and what music has played or is about to play.

Radio is aimed at a mass audience and serves up a variety of content to attract as many listeners as possible. This content goes out live, unedited. Mistakes made live, such as fluffing of lines or swearing, live forever. Radio concentrates very much on what is topical in the moment and once it has been broadcast, will rarely be listened to in full ever again. The type of content that radio thrives on will be outdated soon after broadcast.

Podcasts, on the other hand, are available on demand. The audience will stream or download the episodes they want to listen to in a schedule of their own making. A person choosing to listen to a podcast is invested enough that they do not need to constantly be reminded of who and what they are listening to.

Whereas radio is broadcasting, podcasting is narrowcasting. Podcasts appeal to niche audiences and therefore specialized information that focus on individual topics tend to have the biggest appeal. People stumble onto the podcasts that fit their interests when they search for it online. Finding a podcast is much harder than just turning the dial on the radio. This makes meta tagging and titling especially important, as it aids discoverability.

Podcasts are not immediate like radio; instead, they are like library books on a shelf. Only one person may read a copy of a specific book during a month. Cumulatively, thousands of people will have read that same book over two decades. The fact that podcasts have a long shelf life means populating it with evergreen content will keep the podcasts topical for years to come. A radio show with no listeners is a disaster. Once it has been broadcast, it is gone. A podcast with no listeners is only the starting point. Its download numbers will increase as time goes by.

If you are starting out with thousands of followers who all want to listen to you at the same time, invest in a live podcast broadcast. This will only work if you already have many followers. Having a large audience will warrant the effort of going live, while others will listen to the podcast as and when it suits them.

To go live will require a budget for production and technical knowledge about live streaming. Any regular podcaster starting out should carefully weigh the benefits of being in control of a podcast through editing and packaging before it gets published, against going live and all the technical difficulties that may occur.

How we use podcasting is still to a large degree anchored in radio, where it rightly should be, as long as it does not hamper the medium. While it may be fun to go live once a week and then publish the recording of your live podcast, it is an unimaginative use of the medium.

One has to only think back to the "golden age" of radio when the medium was stretched to its creative limits. Regrettably, much of modern radio is based around either talk or music and much creativity has been lost. Not only is podcasting filling this gap, but it also needs to find its true form to satisfy the very real need people have of listening to them.

When producing one, it can be useful to think of a podcast in the same terms as a television series. It should ideally consist of episodes and seasons, although this may vary, depending on the podcast. There are too many podcasts that only have one episode, because the daily and weekly pressure to produce a continuous, regular podcast can quickly become overwhelming. Thinking about producing a series and only releasing it when the whole series has been edited and packaged, puts a whole new spin on the approach to the production process.

There is of course a place for the weekly podcaster who has produced episodes in advance as a "buffer," to stop them from becoming overwhelmed by the stress of continuous production. They do batch recordings, producing a whole season in two or three weeks, scheduling weeks or even months in advance. This ensures that the series flows effortlessly, as the pressures of weekly production are relieved. It also gives more scope for creativity when there is enough time to properly produce a series.

Producing a regular podcast will require effort on your part. Do not complicate things when you first start out by insisting on going live. It will have almost zero benefit, as you need an audience to justify live podcasting. Start by getting the basics right: find your niche, zoom into your niche, hone your skills, and be consistent.

Summary

Choosing your podcast genre and format will be pivotal decisions which will determine what the podcast sounds like. It will be a worthwhile exercise to investigate the options and make decisions based on the content you want to present. It seems that interviews have become the most usual podcasting format. Limiting yourself to only this one option will restrict your creativity.

Finding the right genre and format will mean that you will be able to plan the layout of your podcast. By now it should be clear that having a proper plan will help your podcast run smoothly and will give it a professional edge. This will ensure that it has a decent chance of rising in the popularity ranks.

A popular podcast is one that people will talk about, which will add new listeners every week. This will make advertisers sit up and take notice, offering opportunities for you to start monetizing your podcast. Having a proper structure and being consistent are key elements for attracting both listeners and advertisers. It also creates audience familiarity with your podcast, leading to a sense of excitement and expectation for the next episode.

Finally, deciding on the genre and format early on during the planning phase will make it easier for the host. Choose wisely now and your podcast will have consistency from week to week, allowing you to have fun in the process.

Action Steps

✓ Decide on a genre for your podcast.

✓ Decide which format will suit your podcast best.

✓ Record a demo episode so that you can decide if your genre and format suit your content.

✓ Record a video of your demo podcast so that you can see what it will look like.

✓ Listen to your demo recording with a critical ear. What mistakes are you making? Does it sound authentic and engaging? Ask others' opinion of your trial effort.

Chapter 4

The Equipment You Need

"A podcast is a great way to develop relationships with hard-to-reach people." —*Tim Paige*

Introduction

When you start a radio station, even if it is just a small community one, the start-up costs will surprise you. Apart from having to acquire the relevant licenses (which may prove hard and dear to come by), you need broadcast equipment such as microphones, mixing desks, and transmitters. You will need to invest in expensive soundproof studios. You will need to employ a team of people to get to air. Radio may be free to listen to by the masses but setting it up and maintaining it is a costly affair.

Commercial radio must raise the money to pay their staff and keep up their equipment. They do this mainly by selling advertising and having promotions on their stations. Some radio stations receive a budget from the state, but sometimes still have to sell advertisements to cover the running costs.

You can start podcast with no budget at all, using equipment you already own, or you can set up a small podcasting business for about $500. If you have access to a substantial budget, you can choose to hire a company to do the whole thing for you from start to finish. Let us look at these three options, to give you insights into the requirements for each, so that you can get an idea of how much you need to spend.

Three Budgets

No Budget

Let us assume you already own a smartphone and a computer, whether a desktop or laptop. You do not need much more than this by way of equipment to produce a half-decent podcast series. You will be able to record the audio on your phone and edit it using free software, either on the phone or on your computer.

There are free hosting platforms where you can upload it to. The podcast host will usually be able to help with setting up the Really Simple Syndication (RSS) feeds. You should submit your podcast to *Apple Podcasts* and *Spotify*, which is also free.

It is possible to spend nothing and still get a podcast going. All you will need is a basic level of technical expertise and you will soon have your first episode recorded and edited.

$500 Budget

If you have a small budget to spend on setting yourself up for podcasting, spend money on a quality USB microphone. If you are going to do in-person interviews, you will need to invest in an omnidirectional microphone or an audio interface and XLR microphones.

Make sure you buy a set of quality headphones too. A good set will save you unnecessary headaches with your recording and editing processes. Most people listen to podcasts using earphones, so use your headphones throughput to ensure that you are recording the best quality sound. Add a pop filter to the microphone to reduce sounds such as plosive consonants or wind.

You may need an audio interface. Most computers have sound cards built in but having extra control over the sound is always preferable. Your microphones may need boom arms or stands, and shock mounts.

Your editing software is still free and the hosting too, unless you decide to go with a reputable host who has an affordable package and good service.

You have to realize that apart from the small investment in equipment, an investment of time will be much more important. Creating a good podcast takes time. Having the right equipment makes it easier, as you get the best quality sound from the word go.

People tend to blithely say, "We will fix it in post," a term borrowed from filmmaking, meaning that it becomes the post-production team's problem. But there are issues that are not fixable during the post-production process. It is much better to use headphones when recording to catch the problems as they occur.

It is better to realize there is a problem with the audio as you are recording than to wait for the editor to tell you there is a hiss on the recording that makes it unusable. Invest in decent equipment and you will not have to worry about audio issues. This enables you to focus all your attention on producing great content.

Here is a sample budget to give you an idea of how to spend your $500.

<u>Budget</u>

Microphone	$190
Headphones	$50
Audio Interface	$160
Pop Filter	$10
Shock Mount	$20
Boom Arm	$50
Hosting Software/Storage	$18/month
Editing Software	$0
<u>TOTAL</u>	<u>$498</u>

Big Budget

The third option is to get a team to do everything for you. You tell them what you want and supply them with a budget. You can choose to which degree you want to be involved in the production process. The successful businessperson who wants to build their brand can host their own podcast series, with a technical team in place to produce the best possible result.

Alternatively, you can stand back and let the team produce the whole thing for you. Big companies are ideally situated to outsource podcast production and have it coordinated by their marketing teams. They can use the opportunity to repurpose the podcast to get material for their content marketing campaigns. This will require a specific team who will be responsible for planning, producing, packaging, and repurposing the podcast.

Startup Equipment

Let us look at the equipment you will need to start your podcast. What exactly you will invest in will depend on your budget.

Smartphone/Tablet

We already do so much on our smartphones every day, why not record and edit podcasts with it too? You will need to download apps with which to record and edit the audio. If your phone is internet connected, you can upload your edited episodes straight from your phone to your hosting platform. You can also take the photos, design the graphics, and write the show notes using your phone. You can do all this on a tablet too.

Headphones

Decent headphones are a necessity. They must fit comfortably so that you can wear them for extended periods of time. Their sound quality needs to be good enough so that you can accurately create your final mix. Bluetooth headphones sometimes have latency issues, so rather invest in wired ones.

Computer

Your computer should be a recent model and can be either Mac or Windows, as audio production tools are freely available for both operating systems. If you do not already own a computer, you will need to acquire a mid-sized one. Gaming computers with fast audio and video processing speeds are recommended.

Make sure your computer has the ports necessary for the equipment. You may need an expansion hub to use two or three microphones and headphones simultaneously if your number of ports are limited.

Microphone

There are two types of microphones to consider, namely USB and XLR. USB microphones connect and power directly from your computer or tablet. For a solo host, a USB microphone will be more than adequate. It can also be used for *Zoom* recordings.

When you have multiple microphones, using XLR microphones will be the better option. These microphones are plugged into an audio interface that connects with the computer. This device provides added control over the microphone levels.

Monitor Speakers

Having an extra set of speakers is not a necessity but an optional extra. You cannot use speakers during recording, as it will create feedback. The speakers can be used during editing or playback.

Software

There is a plethora of free audio editing applications available. *Audacity* is a basic but free editing app. Mac's *GarageBand* and various similar iOS apps are free to use and often have podcast presets. The software will update and change from time to time, so do your own research and look at all the available options. There are paid options available too, so take that into consideration when you decide on software. We will investigate the various options in more detail later.

Apart from editing, the software you choose must be able to mix tracks and improve vocal sound quality. Compression, gating, and an audio equalizer (EQ) will be required.

Podcast Studio

You can rent a purpose-built podcast studio and make use of professional editing and other services at a fee. If you are serious about podcasting, you could decide to rig your own studio for the purpose and employ a small technical team. You will get the best acoustics in a professional sound studio.

If a proper studio is outside of your budget, you can rig a studio at home, creating a dedicated space for recording. Make sure it is soundproof, or at least quiet. Additionally, the space needs to be conditioned for sound. This can be done by covering walls with blankets or placing pillows in ceiling corners.

Those with a budget can invest in acoustic tiling. Unfortunately, egg boxes do not provide much benefit by way of acoustics. Portable microphone booths are commercially available, or you can build a booth using pillows on a bed or couch. If all else fails, record inside a closet or in car parked indoors.

Lighting in the studio becomes important if you want to video your podcasts. Make sure that a team member checks the lighting so that everyone is clearly visible. Your studio might need a green screen if you are doing video. Keep the studio clean and decorate it appropriately. Your brand is going to be on display, so always put your best foot forward.

Mobile Podcast Rig

If you plan to go to various places or meet different people, such as for a travel podcast, you will need to invest in lighter, portable equipment. A laptop, microphone (USB, portable, or smartphone) and headphones, will be enough. There are a range of mobile microphones available; ask at your local specialist retailer or find them online. Pack your equipment separately and keep cables tidy. If you use batteries, always have spare ones charged.

Summary

One of the biggest allures of podcasting is that the barrier to entry is so low. You could do everything on a smartphone if you needed to. The only thing standing in your way is your creativity. The fact that you need so little equipment, sets the podcaster free from the confines of the studio. It is up to the podcaster to use the few pieces of equipment in such a way that it produces extraordinary, compelling, and entertaining content.

It is important to get the highest audio quality possible, so do not skimp on the equipment. Choose mid-range and above equipment wherever you can, and you will be able to produce great audio.

Action Steps

✓ Decide on your budget.

✓ Do a stock take of your available equipment and test it to make sure the audio quality is good enough.

✓ Invest in the equipment you will need, based on the above.

✓ Test the equipment thoroughly before recording your first episode.

Part 2 – Production

Chapter 5

How to Produce Your Podcast

"As podcast hosts, we have to be more animated because the person listening can't actually see you and the audience certainly can't see you either." —Jordan Harbinger

Introduction

There are two types of planning to be done before recording the launch episode. The first has to do with the overall arc of your show, while the second is about planning each of the episodes. It is no use jumping into podcasting on the strength of having knowledge or expertise in a certain area alone.

Knowing what you already know about your ideal listener, you can start to craft a podcast structured in such a way that it will have the biggest impact.

The more detailed your planning is at this stage, the easier it will be when you are recording and editing. Ideally, you want to script each episode, so that there is no room for rambling or getting side-tracked.

There are various script options, which will be discussed in the next chapter. Preparing a podcast entails more than writing a script, however. There are other factors that go into the planning that need attention if you want to deliver a podcast that sounds professional and provides useful entertainment to its avid listener.

Some of the points covered in this chapter have been mentioned before, but because they are so important, they are stressed again.

Steps to Produce a Podcast

Research

By now, you should have a clear idea of the theme, genre, format, and style of your intended podcast. You have created a well-defined ideal listener avatar and have chosen your sub-niche carefully to appeal to that listener.

Now it is time to start researching your theme to uncover the information that will form the backbone of your podcast. You may already be an expert in your field, but you will still benefit your project by checking out the latest information and trends. You will need to find a unique perspective on the content to get the attention of your niche audience.

You should also do research into other podcasts that cover the same themes and topics you are focusing your podcast on. By listening widely to available podcasts and by doing online searches, you are sure to detect an aspect or two of your themes not yet covered, or one which is a hot topic. This can help you curate the content so that it speaks to your ideal listener in a way that excites them enough to keep on listening.

If you are doing interviews or intend to have guests on your podcast, this is the ideal time to research who would be suitable and if they would be interested in participating.

Planning

Podcast Title

Your podcast needs a name. Choose a unique name so that it stands out from the rest. Your podcast needs a clear identity. The best podcast names are those that tell us what the podcast is about or what the listener will get from it. Forget about long, convoluted names; short and easy to remember is the best (making it easier to spread through word-of-mouth).

Your podcast's name should grab attention so that it can stand out from its competition. Most people search directories for podcasts to listen to. A catchy name accompanied by an eye-catching graphic will grab the attention of a potential listener. If you get stuck for a name, use an online podcast name generator for ideas.

You should consider the impact of your podcast name on the titles of the episodes. Again, keep episode titles short and easy to remember. You may add the season and episode numbers as part of the title, but this is not always necessary. Using keywords in episode titles ensures they are searchable.

Whichever way you choose to title episodes, keep to a system that is easily repeatable. At this stage you only need a working title, as you will refine the title at a later stage. We will discuss the podcast title in more detail when we talk about publishing in chapter eight.

Podcast Description

A podcast description gives in-depth information about the podcast to new listeners. The main objective of this description is to outline the value of the podcast. This should be stated in a convincing manner, so that the prospective listener will believe that they will indeed get the value you promise when they listen to it.

Podcast descriptions also need to be written with search engines in mind. As the moment, search engines cannot listen to audio, and are therefore still dependent on the written word to inform them what the audio is about. It will be important to work keywords into the podcast description, which will show up in search engine and listening app results. Of course, the more your podcast shows up in the results, the higher the probability of somebody finding it and giving it a listen.

State the main points as the opening statement of your podcast description. You want the listener's main questions answered from the get-go. Make the rest of the description scannable so that it can be read quickly, with the main points highlighted. It should end with a clear call to action.

You will use the podcast description when you publish your podcast, as well as when you are promoting it, and therefore we will return to this topic soon.

Season Planning

Once you know the theme and topic of your podcast, you can decide on the duration as well as the content of each season. You may for instance decide to produce 12 episodes per season, breaking your theme down into its major topics to cover these over six seasons. The advantage of having a longer-term plan is that it can easily be adapted as your podcast grows and you learn through experience. You may find such initial planning will help you think more broadly in the future, so do not neglect long term planning, even if it is only skeletal in nature.

Apart from all the arrangements to record and edit your podcast, you should also plan how you will roll the content out and market it. Your season planning has as much to do with content as it does with the logistics of how to produce and distribute that content. A season plan will almost read like a business plan, with deliverables, target dates, and budgets. It needs to take a broad view of your podcast and all its aspects, whereas the episode plan will focus more exclusively on the content alone.

There is much to be said for a team that is in-studio every week, producing high quality podcasts week-in and week-out. But let's face it, not everyone is or wants to be a full-time podcaster. There are people who podcast as a hobby or use it as a marketing tool for their business. Breaking the podcast down into seasons makes it much more manageable. It relieves the stress of weekly episode production and provides time and space to reflect upon and plan upcoming content.

Everybody starts podcasting with great enthusiasm. It only takes two or three weeks or a month or two for that initial excitement to wane and for the production process to become a drudge. It becomes tedious and you are guaranteed to eventually get sick and tired of it. Apart from that, your business (or life) may go through a busy period, which leaves you with no time to produce the next episodes. Miss a few and you will start losing listeners due to your inconsistency.

Take enough time to produce a complete series within a dedicated period. This will free up time later and allows you the luxury of spending more time on the marketing process as the episodes are released. Your clear plan will take any guesswork out of what you will cover next. It will focus your direction and purpose, leading to consistent publishing.

At the end of a season, you can take a well-deserved break, allowing opportunity for reflection on what you did, what worked, and what can be improved upon. You can also collect feedback from your most avid listeners and incorporate their suggestions into your next season's planning.

There are however one or two drawbacks to producing a season in advance. You may for instance have access to a fantastic guest halfway through your season. You might want to jump at the opportunity, but if their area of expertise is unrelated to the topic, it might confuse your listener and upset the flow of the series. It will be best to record the episode anyway and to "bank" it for a future season or release it as a bonus episode at the end of the season.

Another drawback of a podcast published in seasonal form is that you may lose listeners between seasons. To counter this, you should never abruptly stop publishing without communicating to your listeners what is going on. If you tell them that a second season is coming on a specific date, they will most likely return, provided you do your marketing closer to the time to remind them.

The benefits of producing a series this way far outweigh the drawbacks, as recording becomes less stressful, your motivation increases, you get to take a break, all of which relieve you from the pressures of constantly having to produce new episodes. Giving yourself space to breathe between seasons will help your show evolve and improve, as you will gradually build up a library of highly authoritative evergreen resources.

The listener also benefits by learning effectively, as they follow your pre-panned rollout of information in a structured form. This allows then to binge-listen and navigate between episodes at their leisure.

Episode Planning

There is nothing more boring than listening to a podcast that has no structure and just rambles on. Like any good piece of theatre, a podcast too should have a beginning, middle, and end, followed by a call to action. Think of your podcast as a story you want to tell. You must be clear what that story is before you can even think of pressing the record button.

A podcast that has a good structure will not only satisfy the listener of this specific episode, but it will also bring them back for more of the same, provided the content was engaging and the audio of a high quality.

Episode Length

While there is no one ideal length for podcasts, your audience will prefer predictability when it comes to how long the episodes are. Predictability will be key in everything you do, so make sure you plan your podcast in as much detail as possible before you launch it.

If your topic needs two hours to get its information across, then let it be two hours long. You may however keep in mind that people have short attention spans and that somewhere between 15 and 40 minutes will hit the sweet spot. If for any reason one episode is dramatically longer or shorter than your normal duration, address it upfront. Explain why the episode duration deviates from the norm. You may consider splitting episodes into parts to avoid overly long ones.

Content that is useful and relies on actionable tips will do well in the 15-minute duration range.

Anywhere between 30 and 40 minutes is the best duration for most types of content, including interviews or storytelling.

Podcasts longer than 40 minutes work well for a passionate, highly engaged audience. It also works well for long-form nonfiction storytelling or when the discussion is less structured.

Once you have decided on your ideal length, divide it into three sections. A 30-minute podcast can be divided into three 10-minute sections. We will come back to this in a moment.

Episode Theme

While your season may have an overall theme, the episode theme is the specific subject that the episode deals with. An episode should ideally have only one theme. If your series is about cooking, your episode theme might for instance be tips for using fresh ingredients.

Tell your story in three sections or acts. Plays and movies use the three-act structure to significant effect, and you should too.

During the first five to seven minutes that make up Act One, you introduce the main theme, the different characters, and the background against which the action takes place. An inciting incident occurs or there is a crisis to be faced by the main character. For the rest of Act One, the main character fails to deal with this incident.

Act Two is between 10 and 14 minutes in duration. Now the main character is making more attempts to deal with his problem. The attempts start resulting in new wisdom as the story develops. The character develops to the point where a final challenge lays ahead, which will resolve the problem one way or the other.

Act Three is five to seven minutes long. The climax of the story takes place, having built tension to the point where the key story is complete. The plots are resolved and there is an outcome.

A well-planned episode will have good pacing that drives the narrative. Problems in pacing occur due to poor planning of the episode timeline. You may find that there are too many events in your episode, making it sound chaotic, without any time to process what was said. Or there may be too few events in the episode, making it come across as sluggish, with too many long breaks before major events occur.

Your pacing will be solved by using the three-act structure. Move between the inciting incident, first plot point, second plot point, and climax, to resolve any pacing issues. You want your story to flow pleasantly and smoothly, so that it is a rewarding listening experience.

Billboards

The billboards are the opening and closing credits, just like those of a movie or TV series. The billboards help establish familiarity, creating a formula that is recognizable and that creates expectation.

Billboards usually have music that set the tone for the series. The same music can be used for both opening and closing billboards. The name of the show, presenter, episode, and welcome remarks can be included in the opening billboard. It can also have an optional commercial, such as for visiting your website or any exclusive offers you may have.

The opening billboard may include an optional back sell, where reference is made to discussions in previous episodes as a way of promoting your existing content and encouraging listeners to download it. Lastly, the opening billboard should have a promise, telling the listener what the episode is about, who your guest is (if any), and what the topic under discussion is.

The closing billboard will wrap up the podcast by summarizing the main points. It will share contact information and list any credits, such as technical staff and sponsors. It will end with a call to action.

The billboards need to be scripted and pre-produced, so that they can easily be added to the beginning and end of each episode. Any episode specific information, such as names of guests or topics, can be recorded later and added into the billboards as required.

Ad Breaks

If your podcast is following the three-act formula, then you could place ads not only at the beginning and end of the podcast, but also at the end of acts one and two.

These ads can be anything from a dry read, where the presenter reads the wording of the ad as part of the show, to a fully produced ad such as the ones found on radio. They can be for your own products/services or those of others, provided you have a large enough audience. Selling ad space is one way of monetizing a podcast, but unless the return is worth the investment, it will be a hard sell.

There are hosting sites that can add adverts into podcasts. Again, a certain number of regular listeners are required, so this will not be an option when starting out. Promoting your own offerings is the best way to start monetizing your podcast, turning listeners into buyers. This is especially true for entrepreneurs who want to leverage podcasting to their business' advantage. We cover monetization in more detail in chapter 10.

You will have to decide if you are going to pre-record your ad breaks and add them to the edit later, or whether you record them as part of the content. Whichever method you decide on, keep the call to action simple and to the point. Do not come across as being desperate to sell your product. Foster the relationship you are building with the listener and invite them into your other spaces, such as social media or your website, where you offer your products or services and convert sales.

Script

The script will be discussed in detail in the next chapter.

Guest coordination & Release Form

Not all podcasts require guests, but those that do, will need to coordinate with the guests to arrange their participation and get them to agree to the terms of participation, as detailed in the guest release form.

Where to Find Guests

Having guests on a podcast is the norm today. While the most popular podcasts are built around interviews, others may only have occasional guests, depending on the content. Expert guests can bring knowledge and variety, keeping the podcast informative and interesting. Oftentimes guests come with their own audiences who can be introduced to your content. This can lead to podcast growth in the medium to long term.

Once you have planned your episodes and know which types of guests you will need for each episode, you can start looking for the right ones.

The first place to look is within your immediate circle of influence. Who among your family or friends might make suitable guests? Are there any entrepreneurs you have met or other of your contacts that you can invite onto your podcast? Once you start making lists of the people you know, you may already have enough to start with. Look at their contacts and ask to be introduced to anyone they think might be suitable as a guest.

The next place to look is on social media. *LinkedIn* can be a goldmine of contacts, as can *Facebook* groups. Not only can you mine social media for information, but you can also post about your need for guests and spread the word about your podcast, acting as advance publicity at the same time.

Online speaker's clubs and networking groups provide access to people who regularly speak on stages, events, and podcasts. *Clubhouse, EventRaptor,* and *Speakers Playhouse* are examples of these kinds of forums. There are also podcast guest sites, consisting of directories of potential guests, such as *podcastguests.com* and *matchmaker.fm.*

Look at your competitor's podcasts to see who their guests were. People who have already been on a podcast will more readily agree to appear on a podcast again to share their knowledge with your audience.

Have a look at *YouTube* users and bloggers who have big audiences and who are already creating content in your field. Do research into your niche and contact those content creators who are popular and/or who have great content.

Browse *Amazon* for up-and-coming book publications that fall within your niche. Contact the authors, who will be most willing to promote their new book on your show.

In time, you may consider having a signup page on the podcast's website as a way for people to approach you instead of you having to go and look for them.

Make a list of the ideal people for each episode and have second and third choices, in case your first choice is not available. Keep the mix interesting and diverse, adding celebrities where you can. A good guest mix will keep the content fresh and exciting. Make use of a spreadsheet to keep track of your guests and the arrangements you are making with them.

Communicating with Guests

Whether you are sending an email or reaching out through the guest's social media DM's, ensure that your message inviting the guest onto your podcast is not generic, but tailored to the person you are sending it to.

Your communication should have the right components to draw the potential guest's attention and convince them to act. A compelling subject line is crucial, as it determines whether the message is even read at all. A poor subject line will have the guest clicking away without opening your message, so craft one that is sure to attract attention.

It is best to keep all communication short and to the point. Start with the podcast's elevator pitch, briefly giving an overview of what it is about. Next, highlight what benefits the guest will get out of participating in the podcast. It is important to mention why the guest is a good fit for the show before listing the benefits of participation.

The email or message should end with a link where the guest can accept the invitation, agree to the conditions of the release form, and schedule a time. Make this process easy with as few steps as possible.

Always follow up your communication if there is no response at first but be careful of spamming your potential guest.

Confirming a Guest

Once someone has confirmed that they are available for an interview, research your guest, looking at their background, career, and other things relevant to your interview. Ask your guest to send you anything they might want you to know, such as CV's or an advance copy of their book. The more you know about your guest, the better the questions you can ask during the interview.

There are podcasters who choose to do a pre-interview with their guests. This could take place a week in advance or even a few minutes before recording. The pre-interview helps to calm the guest's nerves while you explore which questions would be most appropriate. Giving the interview structure before the time and allowing the guest time to prepare their thoughts will go a long way toward alleviating any recording jitters.

You may consider sending your guests questions to help them prepare, skipping the pre-interview step, especially in cases where the guest has a busy schedule and limited time to participate.

Release Form

Not all podcasters think about having their guests fill in a release form, but it is a critical step that seems unnecessary until the first lawsuit is filed, or things go horribly wrong.

Your guest may be unhappy with the outcome and ask you to take it down, or they might be upset if the edit was not to their liking. You and your brand could be sued for damages or claims for compensation made if the podcast becomes financially successful. You may find that there are guests who take the podcast, copy it, and release it as their own, without giving you credit, in effect transgressing copyright laws.

A release form will give you peace of mind in the worst-case scenario. Having the terms and conditions written down, ensures that you can protect your content while keeping creative control. A release form will protect you, your podcast, and your business.

You may choose to start the interview with a verbal agreement to which the guest must verbally consent to. As it will be verbal, it will not be as detailed as when it is a written document, leaving gaps in your legal protection.

Your podcast release form can be a document that you can email to your guest, or it can be an online form, such as those you can create using *Google Forms*.

Guest Release Form Example

As a Guest of the above-named Podcast ("the Podcast"), I consent to the audio and video recording of my voice, name, and images, as part of my appearance on the Podcast. I further consent to the distribution and broadcast of my appearance, including any information and content I provide to [ADD NAME] ("the Podcaster") in audio, video, or text form without restriction.

I further agree and acknowledge:

- I will receive no monetary compensation for my appearance. The consideration I receive for executing this release shall be the exposure I receive to the audience of the Podcast.

- I am granting the Podcaster a non-exclusive, royalty free, perpetual, worldwide license to publish any copyrighted work I supply as part of my appearance on the Podcast.

- I am waiving any intellectual property claims including, but not limited to, trademark and copyright infringement claims, associated with personal or business interests discussed during my appearance on the Podcast.

- I am waiving any right to publicity or privacy claims, and agree that my name, likeness, and business information may be used by the Podcaster in the episode in which I appear and future reproductions as well as the marketing materials supporting the Podcast in general.

- I will not copy and publish the Podcast content as my own content on my own platforms without the express written consent of the Podcaster.

I agree that the Podcaster is the sole owner of any rights to the Podcast, including the episode in which I appear. I further acknowledge and agree that Podcaster has the right to edit the content of my appearance and publish the same in any media now and in the future without first obtaining my approval. I am releasing and discharging the Podcaster, together along with all the Podcaster's principals, shareholders, officers, employees, agents, successors, and assigns from any and all liability arising out of in in connection with my appearance on the Podcast or subsequent reproduction and distribution of episode in which I appear in any medium. Podcaster grants Guest the right to publish the link of the Podcast episode in which Guest appears on Guest's website or app and promote said episode in all of Guest's social media accounts.

Signed.

Recording

You will save yourself extra work by making sure that your recording is of the highest quality possible. Most people get so nervous when they start recording that they do not stop and start again when something goes wrong. It is best to approach every recording session well-prepared and rehearsed. You must take control of the recording session from the word go. To get the best quality audio and content from a recording, you must manage it with the end product in mind. It is now that a well-written script will prove its value.

The Recording Space

Podcasts can be recorded anywhere. Let us have a look at the most ideal options and what to avoid.

- ✓ **Professional sound studio.** First prize is always a professional sound studio. You will always get the best sound quality from recording in a studio. There are bound to be such facilities available to you, with certain studios specializing in podcast recording. The cost of hiring such a studio will be offset against the superior sound quality it will get you. Professional sound studios usually have acoustic treatment and are fitted with industry standard microphones and other equipment. The studio may also take care of sound processing and other technical services, making your life easier. If you were to use such facilities, always discuss the services they have available with the studio manager. When booking facilities, consider doing batch recordings. You can record all four of your month's weekly shows once a month for an hour or two, thus recording multiple episodes in one recording session, and so saving on the costs.

- ✓ **Home-made sound studio.** If you have a room to spare in your house, you can convert it into a home studio. You will need to cover the walls with soft foam or acoustic foam tiles. It is important that there is no background sound, and that the studio is private.

- ✓ **Around the house.** You can create makeshift recording studios using various spaces within a house. A closet can be an excellent place to record, as it insulates and absorbs sound. The sound will not bounce off the walls, as the space is small. A bedroom may also be suitable, as the bed is a large sound absorber. Place pillows around the microphone so that the sound does not get deflected. You want to avoid any echo at all costs. If you have a thatch roof, you may find that the acoustics inside the roof are quite good.

- ✓ **In the car.** A family sedan usually has great acoustics and can serve as an excellent studio. The seats absorb sound and outside noises are reduced or blocked. Setting up the equipment might prove a little problematic in a car and you may not be too comfortable. It is however a great option when you are doing field recording when you can record your guest inside of your vehicle.

✓ **Work office or boardroom.** Meeting rooms can be suitable for recording but watch out for white noise caused by air conditioners or computer server racks, as well as background noise made by the people working in the offices. It is not unusual for boardrooms to be covered in metal and glass and these will not be suitable. Investigate whether there are offices that have better acoustics and little to no background noise.

✓ **Outdoors.** Recording outdoors can work really well, provided you choose the right location. Recording in a park with the sounds of birds in the background is preferable to recording next to a busy road. Your biggest enemy when recording outdoors is the wind. Pop filters can be useful in a light breeze, but if it is a very windy day, you will need specialized equipment similar to those used by television production companies.

✓ **Band practice room.** Practice rooms are usually soundproof and so make great studios, even if they are not rigged for the purpose. If such rooms are available close to you, make sure that the sound of a band practicing in an adjacent practice room does not filter through.

Recording Software

You can use any audio editing software for recording and editing podcasts. The list of digital audio workstations (DAWs) in chapter seven can be used for both recording and editing.

Microphone Technique

Always remember that the better the quality of the audio you record, the better your product will be. It is essential to have good microphone technique so that you record everything you need at the highest possible quality allowed by the circumstances of the recording.

Earlier, the recommendation was made to take charge of recording sessions and manage them in such a way that they result in great audio. If you find for instance that the wind is blowing too much, stop the recording and find a better spot before starting again. It is better to take a bit more time and care to obtain good audio than to curse yourself when trying to fix a basic mistake during editing.

Here are other things to take into consideration when recording.

✓ **Avoid handling the microphone.** Every time your finger or palm scrapes against the microphone, it will make a noise, no matter how rugged the microphone is. If you have no other option but to keep the mic in your hand, be aware of not moving it much. Use a mic stand whenever possible. Care should be taken when using mic stands too, as leaning against or tapping on a desk or tapping will be picked up by the mic. If your guest has a habit of tapping with their finger or thumping down with their fist every time they make a point, you will need to stop the recording. Point out the problem and find a way to reduce the temptation, such as asking them to clasp their hands together or to sit on their them.

✓ **Position the microphone correctly.** Microphone positioning during a recording session is a vital aspect of good mic technique. The best position for the mic is between 6-8 inches from your mouth. Use the "hang loose" method to find the right spot. Make a fist with your hand and extend the thumb and pinkie finger so that you have the hand sign for "hang loose" or "call me." Place your thumb on your chin and the tip of the pinkie on the microphone. This is how far your mouth needs to be from the mic. You might consider hanging the mic from above. When you speak, air is expelled downwards, which will not be picked up by a mic positioned from above.

✓ **Use pop screens.** When pronouncing specifically B's and P's, there is the potential for air to burst from your mouth into the mic. A pop screen diffuses the air from the plosives before it reaches the microphone.

✓ **Do not blow into the microphone.** Do not tap on it with your hand either. You will be damaging your microphone by tapping it or blowing into it. Doing so will obviously cause havoc with your sound levels.

✓ **Set your levels.** Speak normally when recording into a microphone. They are designed to pick up normal volume levels. Do not scream or laugh loudly, as this will cause the sound levels to peak. Always check your sound levels before the time to avoid sound levels peaking, which cannot be "fixed in post." You can always increase the sound recorded at low levels, but you cannot fix distorted or too loud sound. Keep your one eye on the indicator as you record and, when you see levels peaking, adjust the volume.

✓ **Beware your mouth noises.** Unless you are a trained voice artist, you will not have experience in front of a microphone. Most people cringe the first time they hear their recorded voice, as it does not match the sound you hear in your head when talking. Once you start recording, you will also become aware of the various noises you make while speaking. Avoid dairy products before recording, as well as sugary and starchy foods. Eat half an apple to help clean your mouth 10 minutes before recording, and have a glass of water with a wedge of lemon handy to keep the mouth and throat clear.

✓ **Manage your guest's microphone.** If you are not using a multidirectional mic when interviewing a guest, consider using a second microphone. A guest will not have experience using a mic, so manage it for them and teach them basic mic technique before you start.

✓ **Use headphones.** The use of headphones during the recording process will pick up any potential problems and will therefore be of immense value to help increase the quality of the recorded audio. Remember that earphones are an extremely popular method of listening to podcasts, so working with headphones will give you control over what the listener will ultimately hear. Your guest should wear headphones too.

Relax and Record

Rehearse your script before you start recording. The more prepared you are, the easier it will be to produce an informative and entertaining podcast. The general tone of your podcast will determine your presenting style but aim to have a balance between information and entertainment. Work a bit of light humour into your podcast wherever you can to make the learning a fun experience.

One of the biggest challenges, is not to make a script sound read. It should sound as natural as possible, as if you are having a conversation. Achieving this will take practice and skill. It helps to slow down your talking speed. When a person gets nervous, they usually speak faster than normal and then everything comes out garbled.

Always take deep, calming breaths before you start recording. Do a progressive relaxation exercise, starting at your toes and relaxing each body part to the crown of your head. Pay particular attention to breathing out tension in the neck and face. Tension and stress will show up in your voice, so opt for deep, diaphragmatic breathing to stay calm throughout.

Warm up your voice before you start. Hum for a five or so minutes to warm up your vocal cords and do exercises to loosen the lips and tongue. Speak clearly and naturally.

Speak slower than you normally would and keep breathing naturally. It is when one takes a breath between ideas or sentences, that you can pause to think about what you are saying. Newbies tend to be afraid of having "dead air," periods of pausing or even silence, thinking they have to keep on talking non-stop. It is in fact good to have pauses and breaks from time to time. This gives your listener time too, to digest what they have heard. Of course, you can always edit out long pauses later.

Be aware of your vocal tics, those little phrases that pepper your everyday speech. If you are not already, you will soon become aware of them as you start editing. Phrases such as "Like I always say" and "100%", or starting every question or answer with "So..." can become irritating over time. Identify them early and eradicate them, while watching for others take tend to replace them.

Always speak with a smile on your face, as this puts a smile into your voice. Speak with energy, even if you are speaking a little slower than usual. Sit up straight and use your diaphragm, articulation, and proper diction so that it is an easy listener experience.

Your voice should sound upbeat, all the more so when you are talking about serious topics. You need a certain amount of energy to keep the podcast sounding lively. It should invigorate your listener. People are more inspired by a cheerful voice than a depressing and gloomy one. Get the help of a vocal coach if you need it.

When interviewing a guest, ask your question and allow the guest time to give their answer without interrupting them or making too many verbal acknowledgements of what they are saying. Rather give them visual cues that you are actively listening.

Do not make the mistake of using a guest as an excuse to show up you own superiority. You will come across as conceited and egotistical. Interviewing a guest requires a certain skill and you will learn more by keeping quiet and listening, than by trying to overpower your guest with your own opinions.

Zoom Recording

If you are recording an interview using a platform like *Zoom* or *Microsoft Teams,* the audio is not going to be of superior quality. One thing to do is to adjust the settings so that each audio track is recorded separately. You may also ask your guest to use their mobile phone or any recording equipment they may have to record themselves. They can send you the audio, which you can edit together with your own, similarly recorded on your side.

Prevention is Better Than Cure

Sound recording is a "garbage in/garbage out" process. What you put in is what you get out. Record garbage and you will end with a podcast that sounds garbage.

If there are any external noises, such a dog barking or children playing, you will have to find a way to manage it. Know when to stop and start again, instead of pressing on regardless of the obvious sound problems.

The very first thing you should record is a brief noise profile. Ask everybody around you to keep quiet so that you can record the ambient sound. You will need this during the editing process to reduce or remove background noise.

It is preferable to spend five minutes doing a sound test than to have hours' worth of unusable recordings. There are problems that cannot be solved with editing. Resolve any sound issues as early as you can.

If you do make a mistake, leave an audio cue so that you can find it on your audio track. You can for instance clap your hands together or use a dog clicker, which will peak the sound levels, making it easy to spot when you edit. Or you can just say something to explain what needs to happen during editing, such as "remove the pizza story" and then continue after a pause of three to five seconds.

If you need to take a break during recording, do so. Your script will have logical places for it, if you are using the three-act structure. This is the time to save your work, double check for any audio issues, drink water, and stretch out any tension built up during the recording session so far. You can also use the break to discuss what comes next, as well as to plan, review, and rehearse if you need to.

Record the vocals on different tracks and mute your mic when your guest is speaking. This reduces the amount of processing you will need to do later. Always double check that you are indeed recording. There is nothing worse than being halfway through a great interview and then notice you never pressed the record button!

Save! Save! Save!

Save often and make sure you label it in such a way that you will easily find it again later.

As much as you need to concentrate on the technical aspects, you must pay attention to the quality of the content at the same time. If your content is not engaging, your production values alone will not be able to save it. You may still get away with having lower production values than having poor content.

A Word on Remote Recording

In the previous century, the word "zoom" meant to move or travel quickly, or a camera changing smoothly from a long shot to a close-up, or vice versa. Say "zoom" after the global Covid-19 pandemic, and everyone will know it is an online video platform that powers communication needs, such as meetings, chats, and, of course, recording podcast interviews with guests.

Zoom is not the only platform through which this can be done. *Microsoft Teams* has a similar function. Other platforms that can be used are *Zoho Meetings, GoToMeeting,* and *Skype,* to name but a few.

While this software has shrunk the world, making it easy to connect with people from around the globe, the drawback for podcasters is that the sound quality is not always the best. As mentioned before, one way of overcoming this, is to ensure that the audio settings are enabled in such a way, that each participant is recorded on a separate audio track. This will make the work of editing the sound a bit easier later on, as each track can have its noise levels reduced and it can be edited without interfering with another track.

Apart from the video-based platforms, there are audio-based platforms that can be used to do recordings with a guest who is not in the same location as yourself. Recording platforms such as *Iris, SquadCast, Spreaker, RiversideFM, Zencastr, Ringr, Cleanfeed, ClearCast, Alitu,* and *Soundtrap for Storytellers*, all have the capacity to record the audio locally for each person. This results in much better quality audio, even if the internet connection is unstable.

Summary

A study by the University of Southern California and the Australian National University found that "poor audio quality can cause listeners to feel distrust for both the information that they are hearing and the person who is sharing it" (Gersema, 2018). Your credibility therefore depends in large part on the sound quality of your podcast.

People who are eloquent and who do not stumble over their words, come across as more trustworthy. Your goal is to foster a long-term relationship with your listener. Your credibility, reliability, and dependability are critical to the success of this relationship. Your chances of having a successful relationship will increase if the listener can clearly hear what you are saying without them having to struggle to hear you. They have millions of choices and can very easily skip away from your podcast if the quality is not good enough.

All your pre-production work bears fruit during the production stage. If your planning has been thorough, the production process should be a breeze.

Action Steps

✓ Experiment with microphone technique to find the best quality.

✓ Record outside and listen to the recording with headphones on to hear the influence of wind and other sounds.

✓ Learn how to use your audio recording and editing software by playing around with it.

✓ Do a test recording on the video or audio recording platforms mentioned, decide which one works best for your purpose, and make all the mistakes now, so that you do not make them later.

✓ Watch tutorials on *YouTube* and learn as much as you can about the practicalities of recording and your chosen software.

Chapter 6

The Podcast Script

"Don't bore people. Don't worry too much about replicating someone else's formula. Be original with the way you podcast." —
James Schramko

Introduction

Make no mistake about it, a script is much more important than you may think. A good script will contain everything you need to keep you on track and moving in the right direction. A script can come in different forms, anything from a word-for-word script to one consisting of just bullet points.

A script is like a roadmap for your show, setting out everything you will need to record. It helps you keep track of everything as you move from recording to editing. Not only will you be recording with purpose, but you will also be editing according to a plan too. It takes the guesswork out of how to edit your audio. Searching for and figuring out as you go how to best put it together will be confusing, but cutting according to a plan: easy.

Benefits of Having a Script

The first benefit of having a script is that of control. A script will help you deliver your podcast exactly as you planned it. The script is the tool that puts you in control, which will boost your confidence. It allows you to record in an orderly and planned fashion.

A script will help you keep to the time limit of your episodes. You will soon find the formula that will help you repeatedly end up with more or less the same podcast duration.

When you have a script to stick to, you will cover all the important points and leave nothing out. If you just start recording without a plan, you will soon find you have to re-record, wasting valuable time and resources. There is nothing worse than trying to record something of which you are not sure. Rather script it than using trial and error.

Your podcast will have a certain structure, which may need transitions between topics and sections. When thinking on your feet, making a gear change between topics can cause awkward pauses, followed by many ums and ahs. It is best to script these transitions for a smooth flow within the podcast.

A scripted podcast relieves stress, as it will allow you to prepare and approach the recording with confidence.

A good script does not mind if you sometimes improvise when the opportunity arises; it provides you that freedom. You may have a clever idea during a recording, or a guest may say something interesting that takes you on a detour. Allow yourself the leeway to not always stick to the script when the situation warrants it.

You do not need a new script for every episode. You may choose to use a template and just concentrate on changing certain sections. Having a regular format breeds familiarity with your listener, as do rituals. Part of why a listener engages so personally with a podcast, is the fact that it builds predictable consistency. This only happens when elements of the podcast repeat from episode to episode.

Rituals are important too. These are the things that are repeated in each episode and kept short and simple. They create a feeling of consistency that will solidify your brand. Cultures around the world all have their rituals. They gives us a sense of stability and comfort. By incorporating them into your podcast, you tap into these primal emotions.

Detailed or Outline?

An outline does not plan every sentence in the way a detailed script does, but acts as a roadmap with space for improvisation. Using an outline can help the podcast presenter come across more naturally, as it takes a certain level of skill to deliver a script without it sounding as if it is being read.

Podcasts should have a conversational tone and its success depends on the personality of the speakers. A listener who connects with someone's personality, will be bound to listen for longer periods and more often.

Your personality will have to be written into your script, which is a much bigger challenge, because a script can sound formal and stilted and not as personal as it could be, if it were delivered more easily using an outline.

Script Engagement

When you are using a script, you must build listener engagement into it. Use the following techniques as appropriate.

You should write the podcast script based on how you speak. Read the script aloud and change it so that it sounds spoken and not read. Watch out for convoluted sentences and difficult to pronounce words. Keep it simple and make sure that it flows naturally.

Paint visual images for your listeners. Your listener uses their imagination to understand what they are listening to. The more detailed you can paint pictures in the mind of your listener, the more engaged the listener will be. Be as descriptive as you can, using metaphors or familiar scenarios to make your point.

Keep it brief. Make header talking points and create bullet points under it. If you are already familiar with your main talking point, having a list like this helps you to keep on track. You will sound more conversational than if you were reading the script word for word, sounding robotic and unnatural.

Remain flexible about where the podcast will go. Allow yourself a bit of space to freely explore your topic even deeper. This is something you will learn through experience, as you become more confident.

Stand by what you say. When your listener sees that you win your arguments, they will find you more credible, even if you are not playing it safe by taking a stand. When the listener recognizes your passion and conviction, they will love (or hate) you for it.

Script Style

The style of your script will depend on the podcast format. A conversational podcast will have a loose scripting style, based on questions and points to cover under each question. This helps to keep the conversation on track. Sharing this question-style script with your guest beforehand will help them prepare better, so that the interview sounds more like a conversation with a logical flow.

An informational podcast, on the other hand, will require a more detailed script, presenting accurate information that is well-researched and cited. It is presented in a digestible format that makes it easy for the listener to consume.

A variable script style will suit the comedy or storytelling genres best, as the content is not about presenting information, but about telling stories that are compelling and entertaining.

The following simple script template can be adapted according to your needs.

Generic Script Template

1. Sponsor message

2. Introduction

3. Opening billboard

    a. Welcome message

    b. Host introduction

    c. Longer explanation of what is in store

    d. Episode premise and objectives

4. Sponsor message

5. Segue (transition between segments)

6. Topic 1

    a. Topic introduction

    b. Main points

    c. Supporting points

    d. Discussion

7. Segue

8. Topic 2

    a. Topic introduction

    b. Main points

    c. Supporting points

    d. Discussion

9. Segue

10. Topic 3

    a. Topic introduction

    b. Main points

    c. Supporting points

    d. Discussion

11. Summary Notes

    a. Topic recap

    b. Episode reflection

12. Outro

    a. Listener thanks

    b. Next episode teaser

13. Call-To-Action

    a. Shout out social media links

    b. Direct the listener to newsletter

    c.   Any other relevant call-to-action

14. Closing billboard

This template can easily be adapted for co-hosted shows. The various sections and different topics can be divided between the hosts. One host can for instance introduce the first topic and present the main points, followed by the second host presenting supporting points, ending with both hosts discussing the topic.

During the second topic, the second host can take the lead with the topic introduction and presenting of main points, while the first host presents the supporting points and joins the discussion.

This script will also work for round table discussions, as long as you allocate the role of moderator to one of the participants to ensure topics are discussed equally and within their time allocations.

Interview podcasts are really just question and answer sessions and the format for this is simple. It is obviously necessary to write down the questions. The script therefore also must take the format of the show into consideration.

Interview Podcast Script Template

1. Opening Billboard

    a.   Welcome message

    b.   Host introduction

    c.   Episode premise and objectives

2. Sponsor message

3. Guest

    a.   Guest introduction

    b.   Thank them for coming on the podcast

4. Segue

5. Question 1

    a. Guest response

    b. Host and guest dialogue

6. Question 2

    a. Guest response

    b. Host and guest dialogue

7. Question 3

    a. Guest response

    b. Host and guest dialogue

8. Question 4 (and so on)

    a. Guest response

    b. Host and guest dialogue

9. Segue

10. Summary Notes

    a. Episode reflection and summary

    b. Host and guest dialogue

11. Outro

    a. Guest and listener thanks

    b. Give the guest a chance to plug their work/social media/etc.

    c. Next episode teaser

12. Call-To-Action

    a. Shout out social media links

    b. Any other relevant call-to-action

13. Closing billboard

Repurposed Scripts

You may have already written blog articles which can be repurposed as scripts for podcasts. You may have to tweak them slightly to fit into your script template. Any script that is read should keep a conversational tone. Your listener will get bored by something that sounds overly formal or comes across as monotonous.

Make sure to read the article aloud as discussed before and adjust it to suit a speaking voice. Word changes are in order, as long as it flows (according to Shakespeare) "trippingly off the tongue."

Audio Theatre Podcast Scripts

Writing scripts for plays to be performed on podcast theatre shows is a specialized art form that should adhere to dramatic principles. The biggest difference between podcast theatre and live theatre is that in podcast theatre, the audience only experiences the audio aspect of the play. The audio representation of the characters, their emotions, and their surroundings, need to be expressed through the voices of the actors, through sound effects, and music.

Tell a Story

No matter which format you choose for your podcast, your best chance of keeping your listener engaged is to revert to age-old storytelling techniques. Humans love a delightful story and we have been telling stories since the dawn of time. Over the centuries, common patterns in stories and myths have emerged. Take note of them, as they might prove useful when planning your podcast.

The Hero's Journey

The Hero's Journey follows the traditional three-act storytelling structure. Think of any Hollywood film and you will see how to use the three-act structure. Act one consists of the setup and inciting incident; act two sees rising tension and conflict; while act three is the climax and conclusion.

Let us take *The Wizard of Oz* as an example. In act one, Dorothy and her dog Toto live happily on a farm in Kansas. Dorothy's house is swept away by a hurricane and falls into the Land of Oz.

Act two starts with a squashed witch whose sister becomes Dorothy's sworn enemy. Dorothy starts her journey, meeting the lion, tin man, and straw man along the way. Her conflict with the witch intensifies.

In act three, Dorothy reaches the Emerald City where the Wizard offers to take her home in his hot-air balloon. She misses the balloon ride, as she is rescuing Toto, only to be told by the good witch of the east that she had the power to go home all this time. All she has to do is click the heels of her ruby slippers together and she ends up back in Kansas, where she recognizes her family and friends as being the characters in her dream.

You can use the same three-act structure when dealing with a guest who has a rich personal history or is truly knowledgeable. You can break it down as follows.

In act one, explain the person/industry and describe the setback/incident; in act two, explain the consequences and impact of the incident that took place, the effect it had on emotions, the problems and crises it created, and what attempts were made to recover; and in act three, relate the climax, consisting of the most challenging moments and how everything was resolved, ending with how the person or industry recovered.

Character Arcs

All stories have characters in them. These characters can function as the protagonist, antagonist, and mentor or guide.

The protagonist is the main person who is typically good, resulting in the audience following, caring about, and having an interest in them.

The antagonist is the person or thing that causes the conflict, blocking the journey of the protagonist.

The mentor or guide is the person or thing that assists the protagonist, showing the path that leads to a resolution.

When putting together a panel podcast, the host could function as protagonist, looking for the answer to a question or concept. One or more of the panel members could be the protagonists, blocking ideas with their counter arguments. Another panel member can be the mentor, offering more reasonable and balanced arguments, which the protagonist can use to win the debate with the antagonists.

In this example, the characters will have changed their views, opinions, or positions, at least to some degree, creating character arcs.

Non-Linear Storytelling

There are stories that are best told out of sequence. It may start at the end before going back to where it all began. True crime stories, for instance, tend to start at the scene of the crime, skipping back to the beginning, and ending with the conclusion of the trial.

When you have a guest that has made a significant achievement in their life, you can start by talking about this incredible moment, before taking us back to where it all started and showing us their journey to success.

Backstory

There are television series or Hollywood film spinoffs, where backstories of characters are explored and where incidents not covered in the original story can be told. Think of the original Star Wars film and then count the number of spinoffs to understand how this works.

A podcaster can use this storytelling technique by following up interesting topics, characters, or subjects talked about in one show, by going back to them in future episodes to explore their backstories. In this way, an intricate web of connections is spun between the subjects and the interviewees.

Summary

It is a simple truth that the more prepared you are, the better your podcast will be. The discipline of scripting each episode will form the backbone of your preparation, eventually acting as a roadmap for production.

The more time you spend on your research, using the results to craft your script, the less time you will spend trying to "fix it in post," as the popular expression goes. Crafting a compelling podcast episode is no easy feat. It takes skill and expertise to present a story in such a manner that it holds interest and attention throughout.

You must find a way to structure your scripts that work for you and your specific podcast. You will learn which ways suit you best only through trial and error. Make sure you get the basics right first and, once you do, feel free to experiment until you find a way that you are comfortable with and that delivers the best possible podcast for you. You may change your approach after a season or two, once you have experience; but to begin with, use the script templates and develop your own style in time.

Action Steps

✓ Using the templates in this chapter, start researching and developing a script.

✓ Get a friend or colleague to use as a guinea pig to test how well your script works.

✓ Adjust and refine your script.

Part 3 - Post-Production

Chapter 7

Editing Your Podcast

"And the podcasting - I swear to you - on its worst day, the podcasts are better than our best films. Because they're more imaginative, and there's no artifice, and it's far more real." —Kevin Smith

Introduction

A key aspect in the podcast production process is editing the audio after it has been recorded. All the topics discussed in this chapter, such as editing, applying effects, sound design, and mixing and mastering, are art forms in and of themself. If you are not familiar with the editing process, it may take time to learn, practice, and master it.

Editing audio is technically not that difficult. More than the skill required, you need an ear for audio, so that you can make judgment calls. In fact, ear training entails the editor learning how to recognize certain sounds. This helps to identify problems with the audio. Having a trained ear will also help you prevent the most common problems and know when to call in expert help.

Earlier, the term "garbage in/garbage out" was mentioned. This is especially true of audio quality. Once it is recorded and there are problems with it, it might be time-consuming and difficult (if not impossible) to fix. There is nothing worse than having to re-record and episode. Worse still, when a great moment was lost because of sound problems.

Distorted recordings due to too high recording levels, clipping, plosives and pop, off-mic speech and background noise, interference, hisses and hums, wind, room echo and reverberation, sibilance, and mouth noise, are all things to look out for during the recording process. Prevention is better than cure, so take time and make the effort to avoid these problems to begin with.

If your audio is already of the highest quality possible, the editing process will enhance your podcast and take it to the next level. For this you need the right tools.

Editing Software

You will need a digital audio workstation (DAW) with which to record and edit your podcast audio. Which editing software you choose to use will depend on your level of skill. When starting out, there is nothing worse than using complicated software that you have no idea how it works. It will look confusing, and you will quickly be disheartened by the process. Let us run you through the best options available at the time of writing.

- ✓ **Audacity:** *Audacity* is free software that may not have the high-end capabilities of the other software mentioned here, but it is a great tool for beginners. It will take time to understand the layout, but it is easy to get the hang of it.

- ✓ **Descript:** Also good for beginners, this software has editing features that will make editing easy for beginners. It is not free, but worth the cost due to its ease of use. It can create a transcription of your audio files, which you can easily edit and correct. There is also a text-to-video editor, a feature unique to this software.

- ✓ **GarageBand:** This software is free to use, although only on Mac computers. It has built-in features, such as pre-recorded sound loops and synths you can use to create background music. It is easy to use, provided you are familiar with everything you need to get started.

- ✓ **Adobe Audition:** Experienced podcasters who are looking for software with extensive features, will find everything they need to produce a professional podcast using this software. It has audio presets and templates that save time. *Adobe Audition* has excellent noise reduction and batch-processing capabilities, which means you can reduce the background noise considerably and apply one effect across multiple files at the same time. There are many such advanced features but getting to know the software can be challenging at first. It does not come free, but if you already subscribe to the *Adobe Creative Suite*, it is included.

✓ **Pro Tools:** This software is considered the industry standard for editing podcasts. It has a great tools and features for recording, editing and mastering audio files. There are both free and paid versions of this software. The free version provides the basics, which makes it a viable choice for the novice. Once you have mastered the free version, you can consider upgrading to the more advanced version.

✓ **Logic Pro X:** Although not specifically designed for podcasting, this software has comprehensive features, giving you control over both audio quality and music production. The audio output is professional grade. Its automated features will save you time, as it will help streamline the editing process. This software does not come cheap, but advanced users will benefit from all the professional editing features. Just like *GarageBand*, this software is Mac based.

✓ **Reaper:** This DAW provides intermediate and advanced users with a wide range of editing tools and processing effects. It also has built-in plugins, which can dramatically improve audio quality. It also boasts customizable automation features that will save you time. It comes with a free two-month trial, so you can test it out before paying for a license. This software was originally designed for music production, and podcasters may miss some of the features found in Pro Tools or Adobe Audition.

✓ **Hindenburg Journalist:** Specifically designed and optimized for radio journalists and professional podcasters, this software provides professional-level audio, even for the beginner, with its range of automated features. It comes in free and paid versions with different pricing. The more you spend, the more features and recording capabilities you get.

There are of course other similar DAWs available, which you will find through a quick *Google* search. If you are unsure how to use them, look for tutorials on *YouTube.*

Why Edit a Podcast?

Recording audio for a podcast is not enough to make it interesting for a listener. You need to edit the audio in such a way that it tells a compelling story.

You should edit your podcast to make it more listenable, to set you apart from the hobbyist, and to gain more listeners by having a top-quality podcast published.

Of course, you can choose to upload the audio as recorded without any editing, but only if it is of excellent quality and if the fact that it is not edited contributes something to it. On the other end of the scale is the over-editing of audio, taking out every breath, uhm, ah, mouth noise, and pause, to the point where it starts sounding unnatural. A good editor will find a balance between these two extremes.

A well-edited podcast will sound professional and will be a joy to listen to. When the technical faults have been removed, the listener can enjoy the content without any jarring mistakes, which might take their minds offline and disengage them from the listening process.

There are no fixed rules when it comes to editing audio, there are only good and bad practices. These you will learn through experience, or you can invest in training to upskill yourself. You may decide that the editing process is just too daunting and call in the help of a professional audio producer. If you do decide to go this route, empower your producer by providing a script and/or a proper brief as to what you expect.

Podcast Editing Myths

There are common myths around podcast editing which should be dispelled immediately.

✓ **The sound quality is the only principal factor:** If you think that your listener only cares about equalized sound levels and not hearing background noise, you are sorely mistaken. They are only really interested in the content. They will not notice a good edit, only a bad one.

✓ **Your listener will not care if the podcast is edited or not:** This myth links to the first one. Thinking your listener only cares about the content and that they will not be distracted by annoyances are mistakes new podcasters often make. Your listener has invested the time to listen to your podcast, and to provide them with unedited poor-quality audio is insulting. The modern listener is accustomed to good audio, and therefore you must respect them enough to provide the best possible listening experience. Having a long, rambling, unedited podcast, will not attract as many listeners as one that is tightly edited and to the point. Always remember that you want your listener to engage with your podcast, so respect them enough to give the audio a good edit.

✓ **Edited podcasts lose personality and authenticity:** There are those who are of the opinion that background noise, mistakes, awkward back-and-forth banter, and natural pauses, contribute to the authenticity of a podcast. They argue that any editing will create a sterile-sounding podcast, devoid of any character. You can produce an authentic-sounding podcast by editing it in such a way that the most glaring mistakes are removed, keeping in quirks that suit your podcast style. Keep the things you most care about, such as your little eccentricities, but do not make the mistake of presenting yourself warts and all. Only experience will teach you what to keep in and what to edit out, to make the podcast sound both authentic and professional.

✓ **Editing is too difficult and not worth the time:** Editing a podcast does take time and effort and can seem overwhelming for the novice. Patience is required when starting out on the editing journey, and if it seems like too daunting a task, outsource it to a professional at first until you are confident enough to take over the task. A good edit will provide enormous value to your product, so either take the time to learn the skill or get outside help.

✓ **Professional editing is too expensive:** There are preconceived ideas about the costs involved in editing and, because of this, it might not seem like a worthwhile investment. You might start out with only a shoestring budget, which makes this concern a valid one. There are however ways to minimize the cost. Doing it yourself might mean you will have to invest time to learn the skills to understand the editing process, but in the long term it can result in a saving on your budget. Keep it simple and learn as you go. You may consider approaching a school that teaches editing and get one of the students to help you out. Student editors are always looking for experience to add to their CVs and might do it for free or a donation. Another idea is to approach a professional editor and negotiate a trade exchange. You can provide your services in exchange for theirs. Or you could promote their services during your podcast, either as a shoutout or an ad spot.

Editing Processes

As editing is such a crucial aspect of the production process, there are essential processes you need to pay attention to.

✓ **Import audio:** The first step in any editing process is to import the audio into your DAW if it wasn't recorded directly onto it. This could be as simple as dragging and dropping the file onto the interface. Most DAWs have separate tracks, so use a different track for each voice, sound effect, music, and other components.

✓ **Noise reduction:** Most of the software mentioned have a noise reduction tool that helps to reduce background hum, hisses, and buzzes. The buzz track you recorded before you started your interview comes in handy now.

✓ **Listen and delete:** Listen to your audio and decide which unwanted material needs to be deleted. Start by deleting larger chunks of information before concentrating on smaller issues, such as ums and ahs.

✓ **Reorder:** Your podcast may not have been recorded in order, so now is the time to rearrange your audio in the order determined by your script.

✓ **Fixed unwanted noise:** You may want to delete coughs and unnecessary pauses or silences. You will encounter guests or hosts who have very audible breathing, which you can either cut out or reduce the volume on.

✓ **Normalize and amplify:** Make the volume of your podcast consistent throughout by normalizing the audio, manually amplifying any areas that are too soft.

✓ **Add elements:** Once your audio quality has been fixed and the sound clips arranged in the right order, you can start to add the final additions, such as the opening and closing billboards that you have recorded previously, as well as music and ads, if there are any.

✓ **Listen and master before exporting:** Once you have completed your edit, give it a listen to make sure everything is as good as it can be. Fix any small issues you might have overlooked before the last step of the audio editing process, namely mastering. The purpose of mastering is to balance all the sound elements, making sure it is in stereo, and that it is optimized for playback across all media formats. This means using tools like equalization, compression, limiting, and stereo enhancement. Once the podcast audio has been mastered, you can export it as an MP3, adding metadata to the file so that the search engines can understand what it is about.

Applying Effects

Spice up your audio by applying sound effects to your audio. Not every podcast episode will need them, as you do not want to distract your listener with an overly produced podcast. Used sparingly and with effect, sound effects can increase the quality of your podcast. They can be used as transitions, such as a short musical interlude between guests or various parts of the podcast.

Audio has this amazing ability to paint pictures in your head, very much like an enjoyable book can. Sound effects work particularly well in narrative and theatre podcasts, as it explains a scene simply through sound, such as when a character slams the door or throws a glass at the wall. They are also useful to set the scene, such as a subway station with announcements and the sound of trains arriving and departing.

Sound effects can also be used to emphasize a point. It is a bit like using bold or italics when typing text. A well-chosen sound effect can evoke an emotional response from your listener. The possibilities are endless, only restricted by your imagination.

Common Podcast Editing Mistakes

✓ **Change in tone:** You have recorded your content on different days. One day you were in a great mood, while on day two you got up on the wrong side of the bad. Suffice to say, your tone of voice will be different on the recording and editing it together might result in a sudden shift in the tone of the voice. It can be tricky to edit two such pieces of audio together. The volume and background noise may be different too. Take exceptional care when editing such audio together.

✓ **Missing breaths:** Editing out every single breath or cutting the breaths in half is a common mistake that will make the speech sound unnatural. Sometimes two breaths could mistakenly be edited together, resulting in a double breath. The result of breath editing mistakes is that the speech sounds choppy and awkward. Always take care when editing breaths and listen back to fix any such mistakes.

✓ **Spatial awareness:** For your podcast to flow naturally, you must be aware of both the pacing and space, which create the overall feel of the podcast. If there are too many or too long pauses and silences, your listener may disengage, and it may sound awkward. When the pace is too fast and there is no time for your listener to process what they have heard, it can be difficult to follow. A good edit will give the audio a natural flow and the listener time to engage and digest what they have heard.

✓ **Cutting consonants:** A common mistake is to cut certain consonants short. 'S,' 'F,' and 'H' sounds are the ones most often clipped by a bad edit.

✓ **Varying sound levels:** There is nothing worse than listening to the opening lines spoken by the announcer and setting your volume on your earphones to hear them properly, only for the music following the opening to be much louder, hurting your eardrums in the process. Always double check your sound levels and make sure everything is within the same range. You do not want to be responsible for bleeding ears! In the same breath, ensure that music edits are not distracting or very noticeable. The music should be coordinated with the general flow and tempo of your podcast. Choose your music editing points well, using percussive elements as transition points. Quick fades may be distracting, while longer fades may give the listener an indication of what is to come.

Making a Trailer

Just like any movie has a trailer that entices you to watch the film, a podcast should have a trailer too. This trailer can stand on its own or be inserted at the end of a podcast to get the listener to download the next episode. There are three types of trailers you can make, depending on what your goal is.

The "Coming Soon" trailer teases a brand-new show before it launches. It is also used to get a listener excited about a new season of an existing show.

The "Show Trailer" is like a highlight reel of your podcast, featuring the most exciting or interesting bits in the form of short sound bites. This type of trailer is perfect for social media and to promote the podcast on your website. Their benefit is that a potential listener can quickly judge if the podcast is of interest to them before committing their time listening to it.

The third is the "Teaser Trailer," which is used at the end of a podcast episode. It motivates the listener to come back, having heard highlights from the upcoming show.

Another way to use the trailer is to use it to set up your podcast hosting platform and initiate the RSS feeds for *Apple Podcasts* and *Spotify* before you launch. Podcasters usually use their first episode to do this, but the trailer can help you gain exposure and ensure that everything works properly before actually uploading the first episode.

Writing the Show Trailer

The best trailers are shorter than two minutes and are scripted before the time. The trailer will consist of four elements.

- ✓ **Introduce show:** The trailer should firstly introduce the show and its host(s). A brief overview on what the show is about completes the introduction.

- ✓ **Highlights:** Editing together the best moments will give the listener a clear indication what to expect. You can include quotes from guests or details that establish the narrative of a story.

- ✓ **Leave them wanting more:** Is there a question you can leave hanging in the air which might compel the listener to download the podcast to find out the answer? Or is there a story that poses a problem for the characters, or a sudden twist, which will leave the listener wanting to hear more?

- ✓ **Call to action:** The trailer ends with a clear call to action, telling the listener what the next step is. This can be a link to the new episode, the website, or the streaming platform, or a request to subscribe.

It might prove useful to have the episode transcribed with time codes, which will make it easier to copy and paste the relevant content from the show into your trailer script. This will make the editing process much easier.

Edit the Show Trailer

Once you have the script, or at least an outline, you can easily edit the trailer. Use any music you use in the podcast in the trailer too. Edit the trailer in such a way that it is short, snappy, and highly engaging.

Apart from the audio trailer, you may consider adding graphics, pictures, or text, and make a video version of it too. This will help grab the listener's attention. Having a video will also serve as "bait" on social media and video platforms.

Distribute the Trailer

Social media is one of the first places to distribute your trailer. Create hype and interest by asking your existing followers to share it through their networks.

Embed the trailer on your website and write copy to explain it more, with a call to action in the form of clickable links.

It might be a clever idea to team up with other podcasters and cross promote each other's work. This can be a fantastic way to gain new audiences.

Summary

Having a pair of good shoes will only stand out if you regularly clean and shine them. The same is true of your audio content. Editing is how you make your content shine and stand out from the rest, giving it a sheen of professionality. If done well, your listener will not be aware of your editing. A good edit will be deeply rewarding, as it will make your podcast sound exactly the way you want it to, with no errors or distractions.

Invest the time and energy to learn how the DAWs work and how to best edit your podcast, but if that part of the process does not interest you, outsource it to a professional producer. It will be money well spent when your podcast downloads start increasing and your reputation grows.

Action Steps

✓ Decide on whether you will do the editing yourself or employ the services of a professional.

✓ If you are doing it yourself:

✓ Choose the software you want to use.

✓ Learn how to use the software.

✓ Edit your demo recording.

✓ If you are using a professional:

✓ Research the service providers and their prices.

✓ Speak to the service providers and find out how they work so that you can find somebody who is a good fit.

✓ Listen to examples of their work before deciding.

Chapter 8

Publishing Your Podcast

"Long-haul trucking. Just roaming the country, alone, with audiobooks and podcasts, sleeping in the back of the cab, showering at gas stations at 4 a.m., minimal human contact. That's living the dream." —Mat Johnson

Introduction

Publishing your podcast means uploading it to a podcast hosting platform. There are a free and paid alternatives to choose from. New podcasters might find this step a little confusing, as it is not intuitive, and the requirements vary from host to host. Simply putting it on your website is not enough.

You need to publish it to a host that can send the link to all the platforms where people listen to podcasts. This is called an RSS feed, which stands for Really Simple Syndication. RSS feeds notify websites of the latest content and is used not only for podcasts, but for a variety of content on the internet, such as blog posts, news articles, weather reports, and more.

There will be much to do when setting up a show for publication, as well as various steps needed when publishing individual episodes. It might seem unnecessary, but remember, the more detail you add during the publishing step, the easier it will be for your listener to find your podcast when they are searching the podcast directories.

How Do I Name My Podcast?

You will be tempted to start the podcasting process by choosing the title first. While it is advisable to have an idea of possible titles when you start out, do not make the mistake of setting it in stone too early. Remain flexible by starting with a working title and refining it once you have recorded two or three episodes. You only need the podcast name by the time you publish, so do not be over hasty in choosing one.

The name of the podcast is the first indication of what it is about and who you are as a podcaster. Finding the right name can be complicated and may keep you awake for nights on end.

The best advice is to keep the name short and clear. Finding something that is uncommon may help to differentiate it from the rest, as long as it is expressive of your content and precise in nature.

The best podcast title is ideally 16 characters long, or somewhere between 14 and 29 characters. Just because it can be 255 characters does not mean it has to be!

A straightforward and direct title is usually the best. What exactly is your show about? If you can summarize it in a sentence, your title should be somewhere within that short sentence. Choose a name that gets straight to the point and that is easy to remember when people are searching for it.

A good podcast title translates the brand of the show into words. Your title will be a deciding factor whether your listener will download your podcast or not. If they like what they hear, it is the podcast title that they will share with other people. It is through your title that those in search of something to listen to will find you. It is therefore imperative that the show title is catchy, gives a fair idea of the tone of the show, the content, and the personality. Sometimes choosing a too clever or a confusing title will trip you up and work against you.

Here are tips to take into consideration when deciding on the title for your podcast.

✓ **Do audience analysis and put yourself in your listener's shoes:** Remember the listener avatar you created in the beginning? Refer to it now and revisit who this person is and the things they are looking for. What need does your podcast fulfil and what are the benefits the listener will get by consuming your audio content? Put yourself in the shoes of your listener and consider what words or messages will draw them in. After all, you are making this podcast for someone else. If nobody's listening, it is just you talking to yourself in your clothes cupboard, and that's just plain madness.

✓ **Keep the title short and clear:** Avoid stuffing your title with keywords and do not try to cram every topic you cover into the title. Decide on the key message. A title like *Meet My Business, Hypnosis Works!,* or *Let's Talk Content Marketing* immediately tells you what to expect. You want your listener to instantly understand what the podcast is about.

✓ **Add personal flair and attitude:** A good title does not only tell you what the podcast is about, it can also convey your approach and style to the topic. A title like *Sawbones: A Marital Tour of Misguided Medicine* immediately gives an indication that it is a humorous podcast, while still telling you what it is about. It stands out, which is crucial. Careful though that your title does not create an expectation that your podcast does not fulfil. The title must be a realistic reflection of your show, without deceiving the listener into thinking it is something that it is not.

✓ **Consider your cover art when choosing a title:** The very first impression a listener is going to get is through the title and cover art. The two must match. A comedic title accompanied by artwork depicting crime will not match. Also consider how the title will fit into the cover art. Overly long titles will require smaller fonts and may become unreadable. Most people listen to podcasts using their mobile device, so test out your art on your cell phone to measure its readability.

✓ **Do your research into titles within your genre:** Have a good look at podcasts that are within your genre and how they are titled. For one, you do not want to accidently duplicate someone else's title; and secondly, it will give you insights into what works and what does not. The title does not determine whether a podcast will be successful or not, but do look at the ones that are most popular and note their titles. Once you have an idea what title you want to use, see if you can put a twist on it, disrupting the norm in one way or the other.

✓ **Generate an extensive list of titles before choosing one:** Have brainstorming sessions, alone and with others, and write every idea down, no matter how ridiculous they may sound. Have a look at online podcast title generators and see which appeal to you, adding them to your list. Once you have at least three or four pages to study, see if there are any patterns that emerge, or if there are glaring inconsistencies on which you can capitalize.

✓ **Search your shortlist of titles:** As soon as you have narrowed your list down to the five or ten best options, do a thorough online search to see if it isn't already used somewhere else and if there are negative connotations to it. Sites like *Podchaser* and *Namecheckr* are useful in this regard, as is *Google*. Also check whether the title is available as a website domain name and on social media. You will need to set up a website and social media accounts in the name of your podcast.

Choosing a title can be an mind bending experience, but one worth doing. The title can be a deciding factor whether someone clicks on it or not. Allow yourself the creative headroom to explore all possibilities. Writer and classical scholar Edith Hamilton wrote, "A word is no light matter. Words have with truth been called fossil poetry, each, that is, a symbol of a creative thought" (Orlando Sentinel, 2006).

The Podcast Description

As much as the title is a decider whether someone will click to listen or not, the description can be a deciding factor whether your show grows or goes nowhere. Your description will supply your listener with more detail about the show generally, and the topics that will be covered. It will indicate the genre and introduce the host(s). It will, through the way it is scripted, provide a glimpse into the overall vibe of the show. More importantly, it will highlight the benefits the listener will get when engaging with it.

Include the following information in your podcast description.

- ✓ **Introduce the host:** To create a good relationship with your listener, tell them who you are. This does not have to be a complete life story or a rundown of all your accomplishments, just give them enough information to start creating rapport. You can include interesting facts about yourself, or you can elucidate the reasons why you started the podcast in the first place.

- ✓ **Speak to the ideal listener:** Always address your individual listener directly in the description, as you would in the podcast episodes themselves. By now you have a fairly accurate idea who the ideal listener is, so write something to which they can relate. Directly calling them out will make it easier for them to find your podcast and engage with it.

- ✓ **Create an expectation:** It will help if you are transparent about the major themes of your podcast from the word go, as well as the genre. If it is a comedic podcast, tell them they can expect to laugh and have fun. By creating an expectation, you are sparking their interest. This will attract the right kind of audience who will listen through to the end, not those who find that it is something they have no interest in.

- ✓ **Explain the benefits and value:** You need to justify why the listener should invest their time into listening to your podcast. What will they gain from doing so? Will they learn something new or are you providing a unique angle into an already familiar topic? What sets your podcast apart from others?

- ✓ **State your release schedule:** How often will you be releasing new episodes? This is good practice, as your listener will better understand when to expect your content.

What Titles Do I Give the Episodes?

How you title each episode should not be an afterthought. It must be as carefully crafted as your podcast title. Whereas the overall title reflects the general theme, the episode title should encapsulate the content. As much as your podcast title will be short and to the point, you have more leeway in the episode titles to add keywords and phrases, while elaborating on the topic.

Here are six tips to ensure that your episodes are highly visible.

✓ **Use keywords:** When someone is searching for a podcast to listen to, they will insert one or two words into the search bar and make their choice based on the results. To find the right keywords, you not only have to do your keyword research, but you also have to think like your potential listener. What are the kinds of words for which they will scan? Check out your competition to find out what keywords they are using.

✓ **Base your episode title on your content:** As important as keywords are, they are not the be-all and end-all of episode titles. Keyword stuffing will work against you, so only select the most relevant ones. You do not want long, convoluted titles full of repeated terms, as this will put people off. You can always use two or three keywords and add the rest to your description, crafting a title that succinctly tells the listener what the episode is about.

✓ **Use compelling titles:** Avoid clickbait titles but ensure the title is compelling enough to draw a potential listener in. The title should match the tone of the episode. Do not fool them into thinking it is a comedy when it is actually a true crime episode. Match the title to the style of the content. If your episode is comedic in nature, avoid dry, stuffy-sounding titles. Using the words "you" and "yours" is a terrific way to make them sound more personal. Adding the words "how to" also makes the content sound more enticing. You can consider using listicle-type titles, such as "7 ways to", indicating that the content will be easy to digest and useful to the listener. It will be helpful to plan the working episode titles in advance when you are planning your series, as they will then inform the content, and refine them at this point.

✓ **Titles to avoid:** Simply titling your episode "Episode 25" or "Hendrik Baird" will mean nothing to your audience. Even worse is using abbreviations like "S1E24". Naming it for the day of the week or the month you produced it or released it will not make any sense either.

✓ **Length of podcast episode titles:** The podcast episode title should be as short as possible. If they are too long, they might get clipped when displayed on the podcast platform or app. Aim for about 60 characters max, putting the keywords as close to the start of the title as possible. Keep your audio file names similar to your episode names.

✓ **Test and check analytics:** Always test your chosen episode titles and review the analytics regularly to see which ones gained the most traction. In time, patterns will start to emerge, and you can then emulate the most successful ones. Do not only look at the number of downloads, also track the LTR. If people start to listen but stop soon after clicking the play button, your podcast title might not align with the content. This will call for a serious rethink and change of strategy on your part.

How to Write an Episode Description or Summary

It can take time and require effort to fill in every single box of text and add every graphic when you upload your podcast. Not doing it properly will be a big mistake and drive listeners away. Remember, you are competing against millions of other episodes, so the more thorough you are during this part of the process, the bigger your chances of getting discovered. More than 70% of people are motivated to listen to a new podcast episode based on the title and the description.

Weave your keywords into the episode description or summary, as this will increase the discoverability. Include the name of your guest and add a bit of flavour by adding specifics about them, as well as the topics the episode covers. There is no need to author an essay, two or three sentences will be more than enough to entice them to listen. It is crucial to make the first 90 characters count by starting with something like, "This episode explores how hypnosis visualization techniques can increase sports performance."

The description must match the episode title, setting the tone, and creating expectation. Ensure that the description is skimmable, so that the most essential information can catch the eye. Avoid spelling mistakes at all costs.

When in doubt, simplify the text and boil it down to the most essential information. Whatever you do, do not spoil the episode by providing too much information in the description or summary.

Always get feedback from somebody else. A second pair of eyes can help you catch any typos and confusing text.

Choosing a Hosting Platform

Just loading your audio files onto a website will not bring you any results. You need to upload the podcast episodes to a reputable podcast host that has both server capacity and the ability to syndicate your content to specifically *Apple Podcasts* and *Spotify*. There are a great many such companies, so choosing the right one is no easy task. Each offers different functionalities at different prices, so finding the one with the right features for you is important.

You may choose to start with a free platform or a paid one that has a free starter option. Be careful of free platforms though, as their support service may be lacking or non-existent.

Start by analysing your needs before you decide which host to use. You will need to answer these questions to help you decide.

✓ **How much content will you be producing?** If you will be producing longer episodes on a regular basis, you will need more storage space on the podcast server.

✓ **How often will you upload episodes?** Free services may limit the number of times you can upload episodes per month.

✓ **How big will your audience eventually be?** Your host may limit the number of downloads per month.

✓ **How fast will your audience grow?** You will need to consider how much bandwidth a host makes available to you, as more downloads need more bandwidth.

✓ **Do you want to monetize the podcast?** Podcast hosts can insert paid ads into your podcast, provided there are enough downloads per episode to qualify for this service.

✓ **Which analytics features do you need?** You must determine the number of metrics you need to consider so that you can measure your show's success. There are at least 55 such metrics. Knowing which ones are important to you, can help you grow your audience.

✓ **How good must the podcast player be, and can you embed it on your website?** It is highly recommended that you embed your podcast player on your website. Most hosts offer embeddable players, but not all players are equal.

✓ **Will you need technical support?** There is nothing worse than running into a technical issue and sending a support request, only to get no answer. Test the support on any platform before you sign up.

✓ **What is your budget?** You may choose to start with a free service and upgrade to a paid version later. Be careful that you do not have to change hosts in the process. Choose a host that has a free option that can be upgraded to a paid option. Or, if you have enough of a budget, opt for a small package and upgrade later.

✓ **How user friendly is it?** You want the user interface to be as easy as possible to use. Do not use a host that forces you to struggle with code if you have no coding experience. The steps to upload and publish must be simple and the website clean enough to navigate easily.

✓ **Do you have one or multiple podcasts?** Hosting multiple podcasts under one host is ideal, as you only need one login.

Make sure you do your research before deciding on a host. Compare the different ones and read reviews of users. Visit forums where hosting platforms are discussed and reach out to other podcasters to get their opinions and recommendations. Always make sure that whichever host you choose meets your specific needs. Use the trial version (if they have one) to see if it works for you. Choosing the right hosting platform is a crucial decision, so make sure you do your homework before making a final decision.

Most Popular Podcast Hosting Platforms

At the time of writing, these hosting platforms are the most popular.

✓ **SoundCloud**: This is one of the most popular platforms around now. It is easy to use and has a free plan, ideal for the new podcaster.

✓ **Fusebox:** You can integrate this platform into your website, making it instantly listenable to your website visitors. It has a range of features, such as multiple buttons for download, sharing, and subscription. It can also be easily customized.

✓ **Disctopia:** This platform has extensive features, allowing you to easily record and distribute. It also has a streaming feature, which means you can go live at the click of a button.

✓ **Resonate Recordings:** An all-in-one platform where you can create, publish, and distribute your podcast. It also has a monetization feature, allowing you to insert or ad adverts at specific timestamps.

✓ **Castos:** This platform integrates easily with *WordPress*. It can automate publishing, has customizable options, and can aggregate data from multiple podcast platforms. It also offers a transcription service and ease of use when republishing on *YouTube*.

✓ **Spreaker:** There are a variety of plans to choose from, depending on your needs. It can also accommodate live shows.

✓ **Transistor:** This host has great distribution channels and detailed analytics features.

✓ **PodServe.fm:** This is a full-service hosting service with enhanced storage facilities. It promises to "do all the work" for you, including distribution and an embeddable player.

✓ **Blubrry:** This very flexible host has affordable plans and provides podcast statistic insights.

✓ **bCast:** A popular host, especially if you are looking to get traffic, increase revenue, and build brand authority.

✓ **Iono.fm:** This South African platform is excellent value for money and has good customer service. It boasts a modern podcasting platform that is reliable and has 24/7 radio streaming. It features dynamic podcast ad insertion, boasts a themed mobile app for your content, can recognize songs and ads in live streams, and can archive radio streams to the cloud.

Transcript

A transcript is a verbatim written account of what is said in your podcast. You might think to skip this step and that would be a mistake. Having a written version of your podcast recording is important for the following reasons.

The World Health Organization (WHO) estimates that there are 466 million hearing impaired people in the world. By not making your podcast accessible to them, you are depriving them of the opportunity to engage with your content. You may stand to lose millions of prospects by not having a transcript of your podcast available.

Also consider that search engines cannot (as yet) listen to audio or video. Search results are purely based on text. Your podcast transcript is therefore important in this regard. They give search engines the information that will appear in their search results.

Have a look at the most popular and most downloaded podcasts, and you will soon realize part of their success is the fact that they have been transcribed.

Let us investigate more reasons why the transcript is such an important part of the podcast creation process.

✓ **It boosts your SEO:** Meta descriptions and transcripts are the best way to tell search engines what your content consists of, improving the chances of potential listeners finding it. *Google* also ranks pages with written content higher, so having your episodes transcribed will be to your SEO's benefit.

✓ **Your podcast becomes searchable:** Imagine your listener wanting to get to a specific piece of information they vaguely remember from one of your podcast episodes, but they are unsure which episode it was in or exactly where in the episode it was. To find it, they will have to relisten to your podcasts, which makes it a daunting task, one they likely will not have time for. Having a transcript of your content eliminates that hassle. Using a search function, they can type in key words, and the chances of them finding what they are looking for will increase dramatically.

✓ **It makes your content shareable:** People love to share something they find interesting and engaging on social media. Using the transcript as a source for quotable snippets, either paraphrased or verbatim. Easily shareable, they draw in friends, family, and other contacts into the conversation. You might just get new listeners because of it.

✓ **It provides you with quotes:** There are few things as powerful as a quote. Inserting quotes from podcasts into blog articles will give them credibility and make them more real for the reader. A transcript can also be the basis of a press release and graphics, using appropriate quotes that can be lifted straight from the transcript.

✓ **It makes it more accessible:** Sometimes your guests will talk over each other, making it difficult to understand what was said. Referring to a transcript will help clarify what was misheard. The listener can also read anything they missed. When turning your podcast into a video, you can use the transcript as the basis for captions.

✓ **It improves the podcast experience for people speaking other languages:** Podcasts are a global media form. People who are not fluent in the language of your podcast may not understand everything. Following using a transcript can increase their understanding. It is a wonderful way for them to connect and engage with you and your content.

✓ **It makes the repurposing process easier:** Most podcasters record their episodes, post them, and then forget about them, as they move on to the next one. They miss opportunities to repurpose their content into other media forms, which will help them to better market their podcast and get their message across to those who may not be podcast listeners. The transcript is the ideal source material for a variety of repurposed content.

✓ **It gives your podcast a more professional feel:** How do you make your podcast stand out from the millions of others? How do you make your audience trust you more? Put more than just the podcast link on your web page. Create a well-designed page with excerpts, quotes, and explanations. The transcript will lend credibility to your efforts and increase the chances of the listener clicking the play button.

There are countless transcription services available. With the rise of Artificial Intelligence (AI), you can use such a service to transcribe the audio for free. Be warned though, at the time of writing, AI transcription services are still in their infancy, and AI generated transcripts are often riddled with mistakes. Using an AI might seem like a cheap shortcut but usually results in a huge amount of work to fix the text.

It is highly recommended to get an actual person to transcribe the podcast, as you will get a much higher level of accuracy, while at the same time creating work for an actual person, not a machine. Once again, do your research and test various services until you find one you like and trust.

Graphics

As with any company or product, you need to carefully consider the podcast's brand. This will be reflected in the design choices you make for your graphics. You also need to consider the tastes of your ideal listener and what might attract your audience. It is best to check in with your podcast host as to the exact dimensions they require for the various graphics. You will need at least the following ones.

✓ **Podcast cover art:** This graphic should represent your podcast as a whole. It is the first thing a listener will see, and therefore the face of your show. Remember that first impressions count, so the design for this graphic should be clear, readable, and to the point. Choose fonts, colours, and pictures that represent your brand, which you will repeat in the other graphics.

✓ **Episode cover art:** The episode graphic should have the same look and feel as the podcast cover art but will change from episode to episode to reflect the content. This is your opportunity to visually represent the podcast synopsis. You may feature the guest(s) (if any) or add a picture that represents the content. Keep in mind that this graphic will display on a mobile device within the podcast app, and could therefore be exceedingly small, so ensure it is readable no matter the size.

✓ **Website graphics:** You will need variations of the above two graphics to use on your website. You may simply resize both the podcast and episode graphics so that it displays better on the website. You may also need variations on the graphics for blog posts.

✓ **Social media graphics:** You can make a variety of graphics for use on social media, using the episode graphic as a template. Now you can add a quote from the show, or other information, enabling you to generate different graphics with which to market the show and the episodes themselves. Of course, the graphics need to be resized for each social media platform, as each has a distinct size specification.

✓ **Video thumbnail:** If you are making a video version of the podcast (and you should) then you will also need a graphic that will serve as a thumbnail. When the podcast is recorded in video format, you will need to top and tail the video with this graphic, or you can convert the audio into video and use a static graphic, animating it using the Ken Burns effect.

Optimization

To ensure that you are getting as much value as possible out of your podcast, you need to ensure that it is available everywhere, has regular subscribers, and get reviews that will motivate others to listen. Marketing will be dealt with in more detail in the next chapter, but here are some tips to consider once you have uploaded the podcast to a host.

There are online directories on which you can list your podcast, website, and blog posts. Doing so creates backlinks, which will boost your SEO. Ask people you know to add links to your content on their digital assets.

Do not be afraid to ask people to review your podcast. Positive reviews will build credibility with search engines and will motivate those who have not yet listened to see what you are doing.

Getting subscribers is an important way to boost listening, as a subscriber will be notified of the latest episode, and this will remind them to listen again.

Remember, the easiest way to do all of this is to produce quality content to begin with, so hopefully you will implement what you are learning here and steadily improve the quality as you roll out your season.

Embedding

To embed a podcast means that you are adding the podcast player onto another platform, such as your website, instead of just providing a link to it. Most podcast hosts worth their salt have this feature available and it is as simple as copying and pasting HTML code from the host to your website.

This means that your listener does not have to leave your website to listen to your podcast.

Summary

Choosing the right podcast host is incredibly important, as it will ensure that your podcast is distributed through *Apple Podcasts* and *Spotify* to wherever podcasts are available. You most certainly do not want to manually submit each podcast episode to such apps, so let the host do it for you through content syndication. Once published, ensure that it is transcribed, so that you can reach other audiences, as well as benefitting from the enhanced SEO capabilities it provides.

A good host will serve as a home base for your podcast and provide you with detailed analytics where you can track which episodes are doing well and which are not. Always ensure that you choose one that has good customer service and that has an easy-to-use interface.

Action Steps

✓ Research various podcast hosting services and decide which you will trial.

✓ Upload your test episode to get a clear understanding of what is required from the hosting platform.

✓ Investigate transcription services and find one that suits your needs best, after of course testing which ones provide the best results.

✓ Design different graphics and fine-tune them based on how they display on podcast apps.

Chapter 9

Marketing Your Podcast

"You just need one person to listen, get your message, and pass it on to someone else. And, you've doubled your audience." — Robert Garrish

Introduction

Since you have already created an avatar for your ideal listener, marketing it to that person should not be rocket science, but common sense, combined with clever marketing tactics and strategies. A comprehensive podcast promotion plan will enhance the discoverability of your podcast, increase its reach, and grow the number of listeners.

Marketing a podcast does not differ much from marketing any business or product, as the principles are the same, even if the methods may differ. Whether you are producing a podcast as a hobby or for monetary gain, or even to promote your business, you still must promote your show and grow your audience using both tried and tested marketing methods, as well as specialized techniques.

You should be using a four-pronged strategy.

These include leveraging the right promotional channels; creating a promo with engaging content that can be distributed via social media; making use of your current audience; and collaborating with your guests and other podcasters.

Effective marketing will require both time and attention to detail. You need to be realistic about the timeframe required to get your message to your audience.

In this chapter, attention will be given to the most important avenues for marketing, as well as providing tips and advice on how to get the most value out of your marketing campaign.

The Launch

The biggest mistake a new podcaster can make is to launch a new podcast series with only one episode available to listen to. Take a leaf from online movie streaming sites. When a new series drops, they do not just have one episode available, they have the whole series uploaded, or at least four episodes to get you started, adding new ones on a regular basis.

You want to hook your audience from the word go. The television model of broadcasting one episode per week is so last century! Nowadays, people want to binge their content. If you were to launch with only one episode, your audience will be left craving for more, but now must wait for a week or a month (depending on your schedule) for the next episode. The danger exists that you will lose their attention, as they find something else that piques their interest.

Launch with between three and six episodes and commit to your release schedule. It helps to have at least four episodes banked, so that you do not put yourself under unnecessary pressure.

The ideal scenario would be to produce the first 10 episodes, release four as the launch, and then keep producing new episodes as you release your banked episodes as scheduled. You can even upload all 10 episodes onto your hosting platform and schedule their release in advance.

The Website

You may choose to dedicate space on your existing website for your podcast, but there are advantages to having a website dedicated for the podcast only. It helps with the discoverability of your podcast, provided it is well-crafted, and its SEO set up properly, which includes the advice in this regard provided in earlier chapters.

Having a dedicated website makes it easier for potential listeners to find your content, allowing you to obtain new traffic and new eyes on your podcast's website pages. You can embed a player on your front page, while creating a page for each of the episodes, where you can add the transcript, articles, graphics, and links pertaining to that episode, all in one place. Ensure the website is user-friendly and easy to navigate, and your SEO ranking will thank you for it.

The website also gives you ownership and full control of your podcast. You can ensure that everything is on-brand, and you can easily make changes and improvements yourself. As time goes by, you may choose to change your podcast host, but if your audience is used to visiting your website, you will be perceived as dependable and consistent.

A website is also a suitable place to build community. Podcasting is a social experience, and you can include your listeners in the conversation by providing a space where they can comment, share their experiences, and interact with you. By adding a questionnaire and feedback forms, you can get a clear idea of what your audience thinks. Using these insights, you plan your future content around the ideas you will glean from their interaction. You may even answer their specific questions in future episodes, giving the podcast a more individualized touch. The more your audience feels they are included, the more loyal they will become.

Having a podcast website eases the marketing process, as you now only promote the one central hub that is the website. Here, you can add links to your social media platforms and the most popular podcast sites where your podcast is available, such as *Spotify* and *Apple Podcasts*. It is recommended you add "share" buttons to your website, which means your audience can motivate their friends and others to listen without you having to lift a finger, increasing your organic reach.

Your website can become an integral part of your sales funnel. If your podcast is the top of that funnel, the website is the next step. Here you pull them into episodes and, once there, you can have them sign up for a newsletter or free download; giving you the opportunity to collect their email addresses; so building your database. As you will see later, the email database can play a significant role in notifying them of new episodes, special newsletters, and offers for the products or services you may be selling.

The Blog

Think of a blog post as a teaser for your podcast. It becomes a useful piece of marketing material if written correctly and if it has the podcast embedded in the article. The transcript should serve as the basis for the blog article, and you can add extra research around the topic to give the blog post more depth.

Consult your ideal listener avatar and write your blog as if you are speaking directly to this person. Your content must always cater to the needs of your niche audience, and a blog is the perfect place to add value, bringing more listeners to your podcast.

Pay particular attention to the blog heading. It needs to grab the attention, convey your central message, and give a hint of what is to come. The heading is the first clue that the content is exactly what the reader is looking for. The heading needs to be descriptive, informative, intriguing, and genuinely interesting, if it is to grab attention.

Use *Google Trends* and similar websites to ascertain what people are looking for within your podcast's niche. This will assist you in crafting a heading that will fit into high search patterns and help you angle your content to best suit those searches. Keyword searches should play a role in the heading and the content, so make sure you spend time finding the best ones or use the ones you have already researched for your series and episode titles.

Make the blog scannable with headings and subheadings, highlighting the most pertinent points. As you repurpose the podcast transcript, carefully edit and tweak it, and you will have the recipe for success right at the tips of your fingers. Add eye-catching images to complete the blog and make it stand out from the rest. You can add photos, infographics, or other images to grab and hold the reader's attention.

Remember that your blog will contribute to your SEO. While you are primarily writing for a reader, keep the search engines in mind too when writing the blog. There is no use having a great blog, but nobody reads it because it was not found in the first place!

Add internal links to other content on your website and external links to, for instance, your guest's website or *LinkedIn* profile, as this will help build content authority.

Nothing stops you from writing a multitude of blog posts based on one episode. You are only limited by your creativity and the amount of effort you are willing to put into it. If all else fails, engage the services of a professional writer, and reap the ample rewards for the modest investment you will have to make.

You can also consider writing a guest blog on somebody else's site or sponsor your content there. Make sure there is a backlink to your podcast in the article so that readers can click through to it. Building relationships with other bloggers can be beneficial for both of you, and you can even invite them to be interviewed on your podcast as a way of cross marketing.

The goal of your blog should be to get the reader to listen to the podcast, therefore it is an important weapon in your marketing arsenal.

Social Media

One of the easiest ways of marketing your podcast is to post about it on social media. You can increase your brand awareness and get more exposure here without having to spend any money. Your audience can interact with you by commenting and by posting their own ideas and suggestions. This will lead to listener loyalty, and at the same time you can get insights into what your audience likes and dislikes, and what they want more of. Having your content on these platforms will also help you increase your SEO.

You will need a cohesive social media strategy, starting with which platforms you will use. Again, your listener avatar is crucial here, as it will guide you as to which platforms your ideal listener is most active on. Generally, the younger crowd is on *Snapchat, Instagram, TikTok,* and *YouTube.* The older folks are on *Facebook, Snapchat,* and *Twitter.* If your aim is to reach business owners and professionals, then head on over to *LinkedIn*.

Ensure that your branding flows over to your chosen social media channels, as it will strengthen brand awareness. Link the socials to your website and add the website address to your posts.

Your posts should not only ask people to listen. Use the opportunity to add value to the users on these platforms. You do this by making sure your posts are informative and have entertainment value. Your transcript and blog posts will be excellent source material for social media posts, so include quotes and other content in the posts and to the pictures, graphics, and memes you make. Feel free to post other content related to your topics too, or about podcasting in general.

Use platforms such as *Hootsuite* to automate your posts, so that you only need to spend two or three hours per month setting up the posts, so avoiding getting bogged down in daily posting.

How often you post depends on the platform you are using. According to *Hootsuite* (McLachlan, Cohen, 2021), the following are the best practices for the main social media sites.

- ✓ **Instagram**: 3-7 times per week.

- ✓ **Facebook**: 1-2 times per day.

- ✓ **Twitter**: 1-5 times per day.

- ✓ **LinkedIn**: 1-5 times per day.

The quality of the content is much more important than the number of times you post. As always, analyse the results. After a month or two, you will quickly see which posts had the biggest reach and engagement. Emulate what you did in those posts going forward and continue to regularly measure your results.

YouTube

One straightforward way to get in front of billions of potential listeners is by using *YouTube*. Create a *YouTube* channel to accompany your podcast. You can either upload short audio snippets converted into video with a static image, such as the logo of your show, or you can upload complete episodes, either shot live or with a series of static images. Always complete the description field with proper information about both the episode and the series, include backlinks to the podcast's website.

Advertising

Should you decide to spend money on promoting your podcast through paid adverts, it is important to understand where your ideal listener will potentially see your ads, then focusing your attention there.

When advertising on social media, make sure that you target the ads very specifically to reach people who fit your ideal listener avatar. Having ads on these platforms can increase your podcast's visibility, but it may not necessarily translate into downloads. There is a whole lot of scrolling going on and people may see the ad but not necessarily click on it, never mind clicking through to your actual podcast. There is the advantage of repetition, though. People do not necessarily respond to something they see for the first time. Thomas Smith wrote in his book *Successful Advertising* (Smith, 1885) that it takes at least 20 steps before a person buys something, there being 19 objections to what they are asked to do, namely part with their money.

Google AdWords are another option to consider. They are quick to set up, as they are text only, but just like social media ads, are based on a bidding war. Those with the biggest budgets usually win the most exposure. Keywords are as important as the amount of money you are willing to spend, so do your research, measure performance on a regular basis, and fine-tune your campaign for optimal results.

You may choose to advertise on a podcast app, where you may get better results, as your message will be in front of people who are already consuming podcasts. Users who are actively using the app you are advertising on will be easier to convert than people on social media or *Google,* who have never listened to a podcast before.

Each app will have its own way of advertising. *Overcast,* for example, has little banners at the bottom of user screens, while *Pocket Casts* has a "Discover" section. *Podcast Addict* offers two ways of advertising, either on the main screen or in a specific category. *Spotify* has audio ads with a visual element, for which you can sign up through *Spotify Ad Studio.* Do your research and testing until you find a method that brings you the best results.

Print ads in trade magazines may be an option, especially if it is within your niche. Here you can do very targeted ads, although you need to consider that the readers may not be regular podcast listeners. You therefore should add information on how to listen in these types of ads or add a link to a page on your website where you explain how to listen.

One interesting way of advertising is by buying ad space in other podcasts, as long they are roughly the same size as yours or broadly cover the same topics. You can even agree to swap ad space with other podcasters without any money changing hands.

Guerrilla Marketing

Spending money on ads can be an expensive exercise, so if you do not have a budget for it, you might want to consider guerrilla marketing techniques instead. You will need to dig deep into your creativity to find unconventional, unique, and surprising ways to get your message across. Flash mobs and other forms of street performance fit the bill perfectly, or you can for instance release branded balloons at an event or social gathering.

Consider approaching a local arts space, restaurant, or cafe, to set up a pop-up event. Here you can display your branding, give away branded items such as coasters or t-shirts, and make a big impression within a short space of time. Merchandise is another method to market your podcast, as it will remind them of your brand every time they use it.

Whatever guerrilla method you choose, ensure you follow all local laws while making sure you and the participants are safe. Throwing t-shirts from a moving truck in traffic may result in accidents and injuries and is not the kind of publicity you need.

Content Marketing

Your podcast is easily repurposed into other content which can be an effective way not only to get the most value out of it, but also to drive those who consume your repurposed content back to your podcast. The book *Purposefully Repurposed for Profit* covers this process in detail, so be sure to check it out.

Email Marketing

You can either build an email database or tap into an existing one and share news of your podcast in this way. Building an email database from scratch will of course take time and you will have to factor this into your overall marketing plan, so that you collect email addresses from as many sources as possible. When building the database, it is always best to focus on the benefits and value that your show has for its audience. You can then use the email campaigns to add value by keeping them in the loop about future episodes, providing exclusive news, offers, and other content that they will not be able to get any other way.

Apart from using social media and your other marketing efforts to add subscribers to the email database, you should also do it during your actual show. Add a call to action at the end of each episode, so that you can add those super engaged listeners to your database.

You may already have emails going out for your other content, such as for blog articles or content that promote your business. Simply tap into these existing lists by adding news about your podcast into these email campaigns. Also include it in your daily email signature, so that you can capitalize on every email you and your staff send out.

Word of Mouth

One of the most effective methods to market your podcast is to get your listeners to talk about it. It will not cost you a dime, making it the most cost-effective marketing method there is. To achieve this, you need to exceed the expectations of your listener.

It is only when they get more out of it than they expected, that they will become your brand ambassadors. Keep them engaged through activities such as social media posts that are shareable, and giveaways that reward customer participation.

The listener needs to be more than just a potential customer; they need to connect with your brand in such a way that it benefits them to the point that they cannot but speak about it. You will need to create a culture that will make your listener a better human being for having interacted with your podcast. You do this by for instance sharing a vision of how your content can help them achieve a future goal; by treating them with respect and trust; and by being honest about yourself and your limitations, strengths, and vulnerabilities. Once they begin to trust and like you, they will start talking about you.

There are podcasters who make themselves the hero of their stories. For word of mouth to flourish, your listener needs to feel like they are the hero. You can only do this by satisfying their desires through the solutions your podcast brings to them.

A quote attributed to Maya Angelo reads, "I've learned that people will forget what you said, people will forget what you did, but people will never forget how you made them feel" (Tunstall, 2014). Your listener will only become your brand ambassador if you have made them experience a deep feeling that inspires them. It was said earlier, and it bears repeating: **You are only speaking to one person.** Make the podcast personal, motivate that one person, celebrate their success, encourage them in thoughtful and authentic ways, so that they are included. Do all these things, and you will have a person who will have the urge to talk about you and your podcast.

When you love what you do and are passionate about it, it will shine through. It will be contagious. Show your listener that you care and the chances of them becoming an avid fan is almost guaranteed. Every single person on this planet wants to feel validated and understood. If you can achieve that through your podcast, the word will spread like wildfire and your numbers will increase dramatically.

Your Guests

Your guests will be your best promoters. When you invite well-known people or those who have large followings onto your podcast, you can tap into their networks as a way of increasing your subscriber base, while raising awareness of your podcast. Popular people will bring their audience with them, so ensure you add influencers, industry experts, and celebrities into your guest mix.

Get Opinions, Reviews, and Feedback

Get your listeners involved by asking them what they thought of your podcast or by answering their questions in future episodes. These are great ways of keeping them engaged and coming back for more. Their participation will make them feel included and ensure they repeatedly listen to future episodes.

Guest on Other Podcasts

One of the quickest ways of expanding your podcast network is to guest on other podcasts. By doing so, you will place yourself in front of a whole new audience that is already listening to podcasts. Start by making a list of the podcasts that are relevant to your topic that you can reach out to. Prepare an email pitch that consists of the following.

- ✓ The fact that you have discovered this particular podcast and by giving an honest compliment about it.

- ✓ Ask whether they are accepting guests, giving a brief overview of why you would be an ideal guest.

- ✓ Mention your own podcast efforts.

- ✓ A brief list of topics about which you could talk.

It is best practice to highlight why you are a good fit as well as telling them what benefit they will derive from your participation. Keep the email short and to the point and personalize it for each recipient. Make sure you follow up your email and respond when they reply.

Competitions and Giveaways

There are a variety of ways in which you can run competitions and do giveaways. People like winning and getting free stuff, so have t-shirts, stickers, or product discounts available if you have a budget for that. If you can't afford it, you can always consider mentioning them in your show notes or giving them a shoutout on social media or at the end of an episode.

You can create a fully-fledged competition or simply ask listeners to leave a comment on social media and reward the best one.

Remarketing

If your content is evergreen, you can easily remarket specific episodes in future, using the same techniques outlined in the chapter. Remember that there are people who will only discover your show a year or two after its original release, so do not be scared to regularly remarket your most popular episodes.

Tracking Statistics

Always keep track of your statistics and look at the episodes that did the best. Evaluate what you did differently for those episodes, whether content-wise or through your marketing efforts. Learn from your successes and emulate those methods in future. You will soon see what works best for you. Repeat the methods that brought the most results and streamline your marketing over time.

Summary

When starting out, there are free ways in which you can market your podcast. You are entering an already crowded market, so make sure you stand out by having a fresh approach to your marketing campaign. Be original and different. Use gimmicks or features that will surprise people and get them talking about your show. Above all, the content must be memorable and fresh, otherwise whatever marketing you do will be a waste of time and money.

It is important to have fun! Be true to yourself and produce a podcast of which you are proud. Your audience will find you. Just be patient.

Action Steps

✓ Go back to your ideal listener avatar and figure out which social media sites they spend the bulk of their time on.

✓ Draw up a comprehensive marketing plan. This plan should include short-, medium-, and long-term planning.

✓ Decide on the budget you are willing to spend.

✓ Consider unconventional ways in which you will be able to get the listener's attention.

Chapter 10

Monetizing Your Podcast

"Human beings love to buy stuff. But we hate being sold to through the old paradigm. So, consider that when you podcast because at the end of the day, you should be selling." —Glen Carlson

Introduction

If you are simply creating a podcast for the fun of it, this chapter is not for you. However, if, like most podcasters, you want a return on your investment, there are few ways in which you can monetize your podcast to, at the very least, cover your costs. It is also possible to earn a comfortable living from podcasting alone.

In 2021, *The Joe Rogan Experience* was the top earner with more than $30 million. His guests included controversial people like Elon Musk and Kanye West, earning him millions of listeners per episode.

Not everybody is a Joe Rogan, though, but it is possible to make an income from it, provided you treat it as a business.

Monetizing a podcast is no easy task, yet there are several ways to profit from it. The key to success is to add this aspect into your initial planning and not later, as an afterthought.

This is not a get-rich-quick scheme. You will need a sizable audience before any monetization strategy will bear fruit. Your focus should always be on producing quality content first. Without great content you will not be able to build an audience, and without an audience you will not be able to make any money from it.

There are two main ways you can generate an income from a podcast, namely directly and indirectly. The direct way is to sell the podcast itself. The indirect way is to use the podcast to sell other things, such as products or services. Whichever method you choose, your first responsibility is always to your listener. You have to cater to that person and entertain them before you do anything else. Without a listener there is no audience, and without a growing audience there will be no pot of gold at the end of your podcast rainbow.

Donations

Once you have built up a sizable audience, you can consider asking them to donate towards the production costs. You can either take direct donations or use a website such as *Patreon*. This platform takes a small percentage on top of credit card processing fees. People donate what they can and ideally you want them to make monthly donations. Of course, you can also open donations through *PayPal* and similar platforms, or even accept the good old cheque in the mail.

Sponsorships

Traditional Sponsorships

Traditional sponsorships can take the form of pre-roll or mid-roll mentions, and the cost of these is determined by the number of downloads. You can determine these Cost per Thousand (CPM) rates yourself, charging for instance $18 per 1,000 downloads for a fifteen-second pre-roll mention and $25 per 1,000 downloads for a 60-second mid-roll mention.

Finding show sponsors may necessitate approaching companies that align with your brand or using podcast advertising brokers such as *True Native Media* or *Adopter Media*. These companies charge a commission for every ad they book on your show.

Referral Sponsorships

Referral sponsorships are an alternative way to initiate income without you having a minimum number of listeners to begin with. You need to identify products or services that you like and that align with your content, to which you can refer your listeners. You earn money every time a listener clicks on the referral link or when they make a purchase. Companies such as *Ting, Airbnb, Website Magazine*, and *Audible* give something free to the person who signs up and the referrer gets either money or a voucher.

Referral links have the potential of earning you money well into the future, provided the links are still valid. This is something you will have to check from time to time. There is a risk when the company discontinues their referral program, while you are will still promoting them through your old episodes without earning anything from it. This may necessitate you to re-edit old episodes and strip out mentions of referral links that are no longer valid.

Subscriptions

Once you have built up a loyal following, you can consider charging them a monthly subscription fee to access the content. You can set up multiple membership tiers.

The problem with this model is that, since all your content is behind a paywall, it will be difficult to grow your numbers organically. Listeners who are not familiar with your podcast will simply not be able to get a taste of what you are offering unless you provide episodes free of charge.

Another strategy could be that, once you have built up a substantial library of episodes, you put your old content behind a paywall. You could also create exclusive content only available behind the paywall. This will only become a viable option after you have been in the podcasting game for two or three years.

Services and Products

Your podcast can be the ideal place to sell your products and services. This works when you have *Udemy* courses or have authored books, and you can offer exclusive discounts to your listeners for these. Your podcast may be the ideal way to market yourself as a specialist in your field, such as coaching or consulting, or you can offer physical products. Consider creating special landing pages where you have offers that are only available to your listeners.

Another tactic is to sell your own services to your guests. You may not even need an audience for this to work. Use the podcast as an opportunity to interview your potential clients, build rapport, and use the podcast as a prospecting opportunity. Your podcast interview becomes a kind of "speed dating" environment where the interviewee talks about their business and the interviewer can demonstrate how they can assist them. You will need to follow up with the guests after the show to convert them into customers.

Another tactic you can use is to sell the products/services of your guest. Your guest can provide you with an affiliate link and provide a unique offer to your listeners. There is a danger that your show will become a pitch fest for anyone who wants a new audience to sell to, so choose your guests carefully. Always disclose the fact that you have an affiliate relationship.

Merchandise

Offer branded merchandise such as t-shirts, stickers, bags, mugs, and other items to your listeners. You may even include such items for your higher-tier subscribers.

You will need to establish a strong brand for this to work, as people will not buy any branded items if they have no connection to you and your brand. It will require investing money upfront to produce these articles and the danger exists that you will sit with unmovable stock, so consider this option very carefully before using it. It could easily turn into an ego trip, leaving you with a warehouse full of items that nobody wants.

Books

You should always look at ways to repurpose your old content. If you have episodes around a specific topic, consider having the transcription turned into a book. You may need to do a rewrite or add content to flesh it out. You can then self-publish the book to online bookshops such as *Amazon* and *Barnes and Noble.* Perhaps you want to make it a free eBook download on your website as a lead magnet. You may even find a reputable publisher for it. You can promote the book in your new episodes, and on your website, blog, and existing social media platforms.

YouTube

Once your podcast is uploaded to *YouTube*, you can monetize your channel by including adverts that *YouTube* inserts into your videos and for which you get paid. You will have to meet certain criteria before this becomes a viable option, though. For one, you will need a strong following before you can apply to the *YouTube Partner Program*. You will need at least 1,000 subscribers and 4,000 watched hours over the last 12 months to be eligible. Should you qualify, a monetization tab will appear at the top of your screen. Once you qualify, you will need a *Google AdSense* account that will link to your *YouTube* channel.

The key to success is to consistently post high quality content. You will also need to keep an eye on your analytics to see how engaged your subscribers are. You can use a variety of the suggestions in this chapter as part of your *YouTube* monetization efforts.

Selling Advertising

What is the difference between sponsorships and traditional advertising, you ask?

With a sponsor, you develop a partnership that pays dividends now and into the future, while an advertiser is a one-time relationship that is usually of short duration. Consider a brand that sponsors a sports team versus the adverts that go up all around the sports field during matches. The sponsor builds a relationship with the team, while the advertisers buy up ad space for a game or two.

There are podcast ad networks that can connect you with advertisers that may not have any synergy with your podcast, apart from the fact that you can generate an income from their exposure to your audience. *Google AdWords* is a splendid example of how ads can be placed on your website or *YouTube* channel without you having to do much except have the audience numbers that will make it worthwhile for the advertiser.

Inquire if your podcast host can sell ads on your behalf. If they do, all you must do is bring the right sized audience and they will do the rest.

Live Events

Podcasters with a large audience base can earn significant income by hosting live events. These can be either streaming or in-person events for which tickets are sold. Add a celebrity or high-profile guest into the mix and you have the potential to earn money from ticket sales, sponsorships, and by selling advertising space.

Such an event can be a content goldmine, where you and your team can record content for upcoming episodes. You can also choose to broadcast live from the event, treating it like a pre-produced show.

During a live event, you get to interact with your fanbase and, as they post about it on social media, it becomes a unique marketing opportunity.

Producing a live event is not within everyone's budget or expertise, so you might want to start small or call in the help of a professional eventing company to help you stage, manage, and get sponsors and advertisers, all at a fee, of course.

You will have to carefully consider which venue will be right for the event and what structure the event will take. A large team, including recording and sound engineers, lighting technicians, stagehands, admin and merchandising staff, and concession stands, may be required.

Paying Guests

It can be controversial but getting guests to pay for appearing on your podcast may be an option to explore. Again, you will need a big audience and a demand from guests to appear on your show before you consider this option.

When you start charging guests, you may lose control over who appears on your show, as money becomes the determining factor, not the quality of guests or how well they fit into your niche. This may result in your audience deserting you as your show loses focus. Lose the audience and you lose the paying guests, too. So, proceed with caution when considering this option.

Summary

Most podcasts do not generate significant revenue. Building an audience is difficult and at the same time a prerequisite for any monetization. This does not mean it is impossible to do, just not something to concentrate on in the initial stages.

You should always start by producing quality content first to grow an audience, and only then implement the right monetization mix you decided on during your planning phase. Be ready for a certain amount of experimentation before you will get the mix right.

Action Steps

✓ Carefully weigh up the different monetization options you will implement once your audience numbers warrant it.

✓ What will each require? Draw up implementation plans and budgets and include them in you initial planning document.

Conclusion

Final Advice

"I wish podcasting was my only job - I have more fun doing that than I have doing absolutely anything else." —Julie Klausner

A podcast will forever be a work in progress. Your first few episodes will not be great. You will improve with each new episode you produce. If you stay enthusiastic about what you are doing and are willing to learn something new every day, you have a chance of making a success of it. The moment it stops being fun, is the moment you have to go back to the drawing board.

Do not put on an act. Be authentically you. You do not want to come across as insincere or arrogant, but let your personality shine through no matter what, as this is what will create a connection with your audience.

Always prioritize your ideal listener in everything you do. You need to thoroughly understand the topics this person will like; analyse which episodes got the most downloads and engagement; and give them more of the same.

You will not go viral immediately. Rome was not built in a day and podcasts are not successful after just one or two episodes. Get the basics right first and the rest will follow.

Consistency is the key to everything. You will experience lonely, frustrating days and will want to give up. When that happens, imagine that your ideal listener is anxiously waiting for your new episode, because it is important to them and is having a positive effect on their lives. You are making a difference in the life of one person. Let that be your inspiration when the going gets tough.

If you want to earn a living from podcasting, you must be prepared to invest your time and effort into creating an amazing product. Be in it for the long haul; do not settle for the quick gains. Take the initiative by not waiting for someone to offer you money on a silver tray but build the audience and the money will start flowing in once your product is good enough to be sold.

Yes, you can become a podmaster, but only if you start today and are willing to do whatever it takes to make it a success.

If you have any questions or need any help, visit https://baird.media.

References

Admin. (2021, May 10). Podcast transcripts: What they are and why you need them! Transcription US. https://transcriptionus.com/blog/podcast-transcripts-what-they-are-and-why-you-need-them/

Barayeva, M. (2018, August 12). How to easily and effectively manage podcast guest outreach. The Podcast Host. https://www.thepodcasthost.com/planning/manage-podcast-guest-outreach/

Baron, H. (2021, October 22). *How to set up a podcast business for less than a $500 budget.* Www.harrisonbaron.com. https://www.harrisonbaron.com/blog/podcast-business-for-less-than-500

Basu, T. (2014, November 18). *Top 10 reasons to start a podcast.* Tyler Basu: Content Marketing Strategist for Entrepreneurs. https://tylerbasu.com/top-10-reasons-to-start-a-podcast/

Baylis, C. (2020, July 14). *What's the difference between sponsorship and advertising?* The Sponsorship Collective. https://sponsorshipcollective.com/what-is-the-difference-between-sponsorship-and-advertising/

Baylis, C. (2022, June 28). *How to market your podcast: The complete guide.* The Sponsorship Collective. https://sponsorshipcollective.com/how-to-market-your-podcast-the-complete-guide/

Belyh, A. (2020a, October 10). *How to start a podcast: 10-step tutorial.* FounderJar. https://www.founderjar.com/how-to-start-a-podcast/

Belyh, A. (2020b, October 10). *How to Start a Podcast: 10-Step Tutorial - FounderJar.* FounderJar. https://www.founderjar.com/how-to-start-a-podcast/

Bond, C. (2021, August 25). *8 pain point examples from the real world (+ tips for better understanding your prospects)*. Crayon.co. https://www.crayon.co/blog/how-to-find-pain-points

Buzzsprout. (2021). *Do you need to use podcast guest release forms?* Buzzsprout.com. https://www.buzzsprout.com/blog/podcast-guest-release-form

Buzzsprout. (2022, May 4). *Podcast statistics: Growth and demographic data for 2022*. Www.buzzsprout.com. https://www.buzzsprout.com/blog/podcast-statistics

Byers, R. (2017). *The ear training guide for audio producers*. NPR Training. https://training.npr.org/2017/01/31/the-ear-training-guide-for-audio-producers/

Carbone, A. (2022). *What is the difference between engaged read rate and engagement rate?* https://support.politemail.com/hc/en-us/articles/360026342714-What-is-the-Difference-Between-Engaged-Read-Rate-and-Engagement-Rate-

CEU Podcast Library. (2019). *How to edit your podcast in Audacity: A step by step guide*. Ceu.edu. https://podcasts.ceu.edu/how-edit-your-podcast-audacity-step-step-guide

Charbel. (2021, December 20). *The benefits of a podcast script*. Podeo. https://support.podeo.co/hc/en-us/articles/4411871581841-The-Benefits-Of-A-Podcast-Script-

Chiappetta, C. (2022, March 28). *The pros and cons of starting a podcast*. Managing Editor. https://managingeditor.com/pros-and-cons-of-starting-a-podcast/

Cohen, H. (2021, September 3). *50 marketing quotes for back-to-school*. Heidi Cohen. https://heidicohen.com/marketing-quotes-for-back-to-school/

Cole, D. (2020, August 24). *The ultimate podcast editing guide*. Resonate Recordings. https://resonaterecordings.com/podcast-production/podcast-editing/

Collier, J. (2022, June 6). *How do you market a podcast? 11 podcast marketing tactics*. Www.activecampaign.com. https://www.activecampaign.com/blog/podcast-marketing

Content Allies. (2022). *How to position yourself as an authority in your field through podcasting*. Content Allies - Best B2B Podcast Agency & Production Service in 2022. https://contentallies.com/learn/how-to-position-yourself-as-an-authority-in-your-field-through-podcasting

Contrapaul. (2022). *How to podcast for free (or cheap)*. Instructables. https://www.instructables.com/How-to-Podcast-for-Free-or-cheap/

Corbett, Ra. (2021, January 10). *Why it's important to choose a niche for your podcast*. Rachel Corbett. https://rachelcorbett.com.au/blog/choosing-a-podcast-niche/

Dear Media. (2021, September 17). *How to write a good podcast description*. Dear Media - New Way to Podcast. https://dearmedia.com/how-to-write-a-good-podcast-description/

Disctopia. (2022, March 22). *10 most popular podcast platforms for 2022 (plus free podcast hosting options)*. Disctopia.com. https://disctopia.com/10-most-popular-podcast-platforms-for-2022/

Dye, E. (2019, February 8). *How to choose a niche for your podcast (before you start)*. Enterprise Podcast Network - EPN. https://epodcastnetwork.com/how-to-choose-a-niche-for-your-podcast-before-you-start/

EliteGS. (2019, October 18). *8 reasons why you need podcast transcription*. Elite Office Solutions. https://eliteofficesolutions.com/blog/media-transcription/podcast-transcription/8-reasons-why-you-need-podcast-transcription/

Forster, L. (2022a, January 17). *5 well-crafted podcast description examples to follow*. Amplify by MatchMaker.fm. https://amplify.matchmaker.fm/podcast-description-examples/

Forster, L. (2022b, February 8). *5 podcast script templates for planning your episodes*. Amplify by MatchMaker.fm. https://amplify.matchmaker.fm/podcast-script-templates/

Fouche, K. (2021, June 24). *How to drive website traffic with podcasting for your business*. Blog.pixelfish.com.au. https://blog.pixelfish.com.au/how-to-drive-website-traffic-with-podcasting-for-your-business

Gaffin, H. (2021, October 13). *Three graphics your podcast needs*. Gaffin Creative. https://gaffincreative.com/three-graphics-your-podcast-needs/

Genres List. (2021, November 9). *Podcast genres list*. Www.genreslist.com. https://www.genreslist.com/podcast-genres-list/

Gersema, E. (2018, April 17). *The quality of audio influences whether you believe what you hear*. USC News. https://news.usc.edu/141042/why-we-believe-something-audio-sound-quality/

Gould, C. (2022, September 12). *How to market your podcast: A strategy for success*. Podcast Production Services | Lower Street. https://lowerstreet.co/how-to/market-your-podcast

Grantham, V. (2021, July 13). *Why your podcast needs an ideal listener avatar (and how to create one)*. Parler. https://weareparler.co/podette/why-your-podcast-needs-an-ideal-listener-avatar-and-how-to-create-one

Guidry, G. (2021, November 29). *How to name a podcast: 7 tips and strategies to find the perfect title*. Podchaser. https://www.podchaser.com/articles/resources/the-secret-strategies-to-naming-a-podcast

Hammer, D. (2018, August 28). *Podcast script 101: Everything you need to know*. Castos. https://castos.com/podcast-script/

Hammer, D. (2019, July 23). *Podcast recording tips for polished, professional episodes*. Castos. https://castos.com/podcast-recording-tips/

Hammer, D. (2021, September 8). *How to find the perfect podcast niche (8 considerations)*. Castos. https://castos.com/podcast-niche/

Hammer, D. (2022, February 9). *Podcast release form: Why and when to use them for guests*. Castos. https://castos.com/podcast-release-form-guest/

Hammersley, B. (2004, February 12). *Audible revolution*. The Guardian; The Guardian. https://www.theguardian.com/media/2004/feb/12/broadcasting.digitalmedia

Hearn, P. S. (2019, December 2). *What does embed mean?* Lifewire. https://www.lifewire.com/what-does-embed-mean-4773663

Hewitt, C. (2019, August 21). *How to define your ideal podcast listener*. Castos. https://castos.com/define-podcast-audience/

Hewitt, C. (2021, May 10). *How to produce a podcast: The complete guide to podcast production*. Castos. https://castos.com/podcast-production/

Horn, J. (2020, July 21). *How to write stand-out blogs for your podcast*. We Edit Podcasts. https://www.weeditpodcasts.com/how-to-write-stand-out-blogs-for-your-podcast/

Horn, J. (2021, January 26). *The top 10 different types of podcast formats*. We Edit Podcasts. https://www.weeditpodcasts.com/10-different-types-of-podcast-formats/

Indeed Editorial Team. (2021, May 13). *20 targeting questions to understand your target audience*. Indeed Career Guide. https://www.indeed.com/career-advice/career-development/targeting-questions

Indeed Editorial Team. (2022, September 13). *How to monetize a YouTube video in 6 steps (with steps)*. Indeed. https://www.indeed.com/career-advice/pay-salary/how-to-monetize-*YouTube*-video

iZotope. (2018, February 7). *10 tips for mastering if you're not a mastering engineer*. IZotope. https://www.izotope.com/en/learn/10-tips-for-mastering-if-you-are-not-a-mastering-engineer.html

Jackson, D. (2020, August 17). *Charging your guest an "appearance fee" on your podcast*. School of Podcasting - Learn "How to Podcast" with Podcast Coach Dave Jackson. https://schoolofpodcasting.com/charging-a-guest-appearance-fee-on-your-podcast/

James. (2022). *The why & how of podcasting in seasons*. Podcast.co. https://blog.podcast.co/create/podcasting-in-seasons

Jaworski, R. (2020, November 16). *Report: How users are engaging with audio content and audio ads in 2020*. Trinityaudio. https://www.trinityaudio.ai/report-how-users-are-engaging-with-audio-content-and-audio-ads-in-2020

Jones, H. (2022, February 25). *Beginner's guide: How to set up a podcast studio for $500*. MusicTech. https://musictech.com/guides/essential-guide/beginners-guide-how-to-set-up-a-podcast-studio-for-500/

Land, C. (2021, March 15). *How to plan podcast episode structure in 10 easy steps*. Improve Podcast. https://improvepodcast.com/9-key-tips-on-how-to-plan-podcast-episodes/

Land, C. (2022a). *How to choose a podcast hosting? Best choices in 2022*. Improve Podcast. https://improvepodcast.com/how-to-choose-podcast-hosting/#Read_next

Land, C. (2022b). *Implement personas in podcasting to get 80% more business*. Improve Podcast. https://improvepodcast.com/listener-personas/

Landr. (2019). *What is mastering?* LANDR. https://www.landr.com/what-is-mastering

Lavender, N. (2022, February 2). *The best advice for aspiring podcasters*. Squadcast.fm. https://squadcast.fm/blog/best-advice-for-aspiring-podcasters/

Lee, K. (2016, September 20). *How to promote your new podcast: 10 effective strategies to try*. Buffer Library. https://buffer.com/library/promote-a-podcast/#8-run-a-giveaway-contest

Loper, N. (2020, November 21). *12 ways to monetize a podcast: Plus my actual results*. Side Hustle Nation. https://www.sidehustlenation.com/monetize-a-podcast/

Loper, N., & Elledge, J. (2019, November 14). *Podcast prospecting: How to get more clients ... by interviewing them*. Side Hustle Nation.

https://www.sidehustlenation.com/podcast-prospecting-how-to-get-more-clients-by-interviewing-them/

Luxe, C. (2020, August 12). *17 reasons to start a podcast*. InspireFirst. https://medium.com/inspirefirst/17-reasons-why-now-is-the-best-time-to-start-a-podcast-da1e0f84f0a8

Machua, A. N. (2022, August 19). *How to choose a podcast hosting platform*. Www.linkedin.com. https://www.linkedin.com/pulse/how-choose-podcast-hosting-platform-afripods-ab/

Make the next great podcast trailer. (2022). Apple.com. https://podcasters.apple.com/support/869-featured-make-the-next-great-podcast-trailer

Marinelli, L. (2020, September 16). *How to promote your podcast via email*. Wistia. https://wistia.com/learn/marketing/how-to-promote-podcast-with-email#build-a-list-of-subscribers-for-your-show

Marketing Charts. (2018, August 2). *Here are the most popular podcast genres*. Marketing Charts. https://www.marketingcharts.com/industries/media-and-entertainment-105211

McLachlan, S., & Cohen, B. (2021, June 16). *How often to post to social media in 2022*. Hootsuite. https://blog.hootsuite.com/how-often-to-post-on-social-media/

McLean, M. (2021, September 8). *Podcast episode titles: How should I name my episodes?* The Podcast Host. https://www.thepodcasthost.com/planning/podcast-episode-titles/

McLean, M. (2022, February 12). *Where to advertise your podcast*. The Podcast Host. https://www.thepodcasthost.com/promotion/podcast-advertising/

MediaEquipt. (2020, September 6). *How to get podcast guests.* Mediaequipt.com. https://www.mediaequipt.com/how-to-get-podcast-guests/

Memon, M. (2021, February 9). *10 ways to use your blogs and podcasts together.* Databox. https://databox.com/blog-and-podcast

Mikutel, S. (2021). *Podcast descriptions: How to write an excellent episode summary that gets you discovered.* Sarah Mikutel.

https://sarahmikutel.com/how-to-podcast/how-to-create-excellent-podcast-episode-description

Milewski, K. (2021, July 23). *Why (and how) you should use sound effects in your podcast.* The World's Audio.

https://live365.com/blog/why-and-how-you-should-use-sound-effects-in-your-podcast/

Morris, J. (2015, April 14). *The single most important reason why you should start a podcast.* Copyblogger. https://copyblogger.com/why-start-podcast/

Morton, H. (2022). *How to edit a podcast: Audio levels, content, tips, trailers & more.* Podcast Production Services | Lower Street. https://lowerstreet.co/how-to/edit-a-podcast

Nelson-Wolter, M. (2019, May 13). *The value of voice: Why video and audio content are on the rise.* Trint.

https://trint.com/resources/q4kpn21r/value-of-voice-why-video-and-audio-content-is-on-the-rise

Newman, N. (2019, May 24). *Podcasts: Who, why, what, and where?* Reuters Institute Digital News Report.

https://www.digitalnewsreport.org/survey/2019/podcasts-who-why-what-and-where/

Orlando Sentinel. (2006, April 12). *A matter of opinion.* Orlando Sentinel. https://www.orlandosentinel.com/news/os-xpm-2006-04-12-free-story.html

Osburn, W. (2020, July 19). *The Best quiet places to record a podcast: Our guide*. Theseasonedpodcaster.com. https://www.theseasonedpodcaster.com/how-to-guides/best-quiet-places-to-record-a-podcast/#outdoors

Phillips, G. (2021, April 1). *The top 10 richest podcasters of 2021*. TheRichest. https://www.therichest.com/rich-powerful/richest-podcasters-2021/

Podcast.co. (2022). *15 microphone techniques you should be using*. Podcast.co. https://blog.podcast.co/create/microphone-techniques

Podcastle Team. (2021, June 30). *How to name your podcast*. Podcastle Blog. https://podcastle.ai/blog/how-to-name-your-podcast/

Polymash. (2021, March 17). *The complete guide to how to choose a podcast niche and genre*. Polymash. https://polymash.com/podcast-niche/

Post, G. (2016, March 21). *Ten steps to starting a podcast*. Duct Tape Marketing; Duct Tape Marketing. https://ducttapemarketing.com/ten-steps-starting-podcast/

Quotlr. (2022). *Podcasting quotes*. Quotlr.com. https://quotlr.com/quotes-about-podcasting

Rashidi, F. (2021, January 13). *Podcast marketing: How to promote a podcast in 2022*. Respona. https://respona.com/blog/podcast-marketing/#toc-item-0-what-is-podcast-marketing-and-why-is-it-important

Raviv, R. (2020, June 18). *Podcast script writing tips: Improving how you interact with listeners*. Podblade. https://podblade.com/podcast-script/#Paint_Visual_Images_For_Your_Listeners

Riverside.fm Team. (2022, June 26). *Podcast editing software: Which one to choose in 2022*. Riverside.fm. https://riverside.fm/blog/podcast-editing-software

Rokk, K. (2015, February 16). *5 reasons why podcasting is important to your business*. StrengthInBusiness.

https://www.strengthinbusiness.com/reasons-why-podcasting-is-important/

Santo, A. (2021, March 2). *8 types of podcasts: The complete guide to audio content marketing*. Brafton. https://www.brafton.com/blog/video-marketing/types-of-podcasts/

Saraswati, G. (2022, May 18). *How to nurture the intimate nature of podcasts with your audience*. Rolling Stone. https://www.rollingstone.com/culture-council/articles/how-nurture-the-intimate-nature-of-podcasts-with-your-audience-1354591/

Sharma, P. (2020, December 9). *How the podcast industry found a voice during the COVID-19 pandemic*. Entrepreneur. https://www.entrepreneur.com/article/361254

Shaw, L. (2015, May 6). *Podcast professors finding your niche*. Www.*YouTube*.com. https://www.*YouTube*.com/watch?v=tDSFT_DCNKE&t=10s

Shea, E. (2020, December 22). *Podcasting is exploding. How do you know if it's right for your brand?* Forbes. https://www.forbes.com/sites/forbescommunicationscouncil/2020/12/22/podcasting-is-exploding-how-do-you-know-if-its-right-for-your-brand/

Shenton, L. (2015). *4 differences between live radio and podcasting*. Radio.co. https://radio.co/blog/differences-between-live-radio-and-podcasting

Shewan, D. (2020, May 1). *Pain points: A guide to finding & solving your customers' problems*. Www.wordstream.com. https://www.wordstream.com/blog/ws/2018/02/28/pain-points

Skinner, O. (2020, July 21). *The complete history of podcasts*. Voices.com. https://www.voices.com/blog/history-of-podcasts/

Smith, T. (1885). *Successful advertising: Its secrets explained*. Smith's Printers.

Star, J. (2020, August 12). *How to write a blog post for your podcast.* Jasmine Star. https://jasminestar.com/how-to-write-a-blog-post-for-your-podcast/

The Oracles. (2018, November 24). *6 ways to use word-of-mouth marketing to promote your brand.* StartupNation. https://startupnation.com/grow-your-business/word-mouth-marketing-promote-brand/

Tobitt, C. (2022, March 16). *Why niche podcasts with small audiences can make six-figures.* Press Gazette. https://pressgazette.co.uk/why-niche-podcasts-can-make-money/

Tunstall, E. D. (2014, May 29). *How Maya Angelou made me feel.* The Conversation. https://theconversation.com/how-maya-angelou-made-me-feel-27328

van Heerden, C. (2018, November 8). *7 reasons why your podcast needs a website.* We Edit Podcasts. https://www.weeditpodcasts.com/7-reasons-why-your-podcast-needs-a-website/

Vissers, J. (2020, April 8). *Monetize your podcast with these 10 proven methods.* Merchant Maverick. https://www.merchantmaverick.com/monetize-podcast/

Way, 20 B. (2019, January 21). *Podcast events: How to put on a live podcast event.* 20 Bedford Way. https://20bedfordway.com/news/podcast-events/

Wendistry. (2022, March 23). *What graphics do you need for your podcast?* Www.linkedin.com. https://www.linkedin.com/pulse/what-graphics-do-you-need-your-podcast-wendistry/

Wilson, K. (2020, February 26). *Guerrilla marketing for podcasters.* The Podcast Host. https://www.thepodcasthost.com/niche-case-study/guerrilla-marketing-for-podcasters/

Winn, R. (2019, May). *2021 podcast stats & facts (New research from Apr 2021).* Podcast Insights®. https://www.podcastinsights.com/podcast-statistics/

References

Winn, R. (2022, April 20). *Here's the best podcast recording software for Mac & PC*. Podcast Insights®. https://www.podcastinsights.com/best-podcast-recording-software/

Wise Famous Quotes. (2022). *Podcasting quotes: top 9 famous quotes about Podcasting*. Wisefamousquotes.com. https://www.wisefamousquotes.com/quotes-about-podcasting/

Index

www.ingramcontent.com/pod-product-compliance
Lightning Source LLC
Chambersburg PA
CBHW031219050326
40689CB00009B/1400